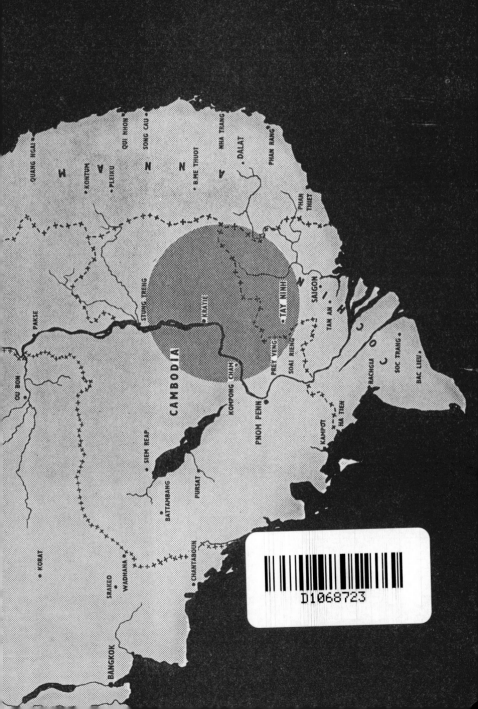

In Order To Die

Henry Ainley

In Order To Die

Drawings by

FELIKS TOPOLSKI

London

BURKE

First published 1955

For

ISABELLE

Burke Publishing Co. Ltd.
55 Britton Street, London, E.C.1
Printed by the Ditchling Press Ltd.
Ditchling, Sussex

Contents

*I*llustrations

MAPS

The shaded area on the endpapers is
the scene of the author's experiences.

Foreword

GEOGRAPHICALLY, politically and economically Indochina was, and is, complex. Annam, the core of the country, is the hereditary kingdom of Bao Dai, and coupled with Tonkin and Cochinchina forms the state of Vietnam, of which Bao Dai is the political head.

The whole extent of the country is formed by the associated states of Vietnam, Cambodia and Laos, which by treaty or conquest have become the French colony of Indochina.

Ho Chi Minh, a communising nationalist, revolted against the French in 1946. The King of Cambodia would have liked to get rid of the French, settle with Ho Chi Minh and regain his complete autonomy. The King of Laos wanted peace. Bao Dai of the state of Vietnam, a puppet placed into power by the French, had difficulties in making any headway, Tonkin and Cochinchina being bitterly opposed to his domination.

The French, who built up enormous rice and rubber empires as well as many subsidiary businesses of considerable importance, tried to oust Ho Chi Minh and at the same time keep their affairs on a paying basis; neither with marked success. Tonkin, which is the rice-bowl of South-East Asia, was almost entirely in communist hands, Cochinchina, where the main rubber interests lie, was in a state of perpetual upheaval, and the French Expeditionary Force could barely hold its own against the Ho Chi Minh rebels. Added to which the French people had been, as a whole, against the continuation of the war and had for years been trying to force the government to come to terms.

In space and time this book deals with the Southern Indochinese province of Cochinchina from 1951 to 1953. Let it be understood, however, that the pacification of Cochinchina has been an integral part of the Indochinese war since 1946 and that, even though the major battles and large-scale actions took place in the Northern province of Tonkin, the overall attitude of the French towards the native population was the same throughout Indochina. The problems were inherently similar in the North and the South; though the communist menace was universal, it was more concentrated in Tonkin than in any other province.

The Viet Minh was everywhere and nowhere. It was impossible to pin him down. It was rare in the provinces outside Tonkin for him to manifest himself in force or seek open combat. More often than not a fanatical believer in Ho Chi Minh, he suffered in silence when caught, or else rallied to the French cause and went on to sabotage from the interior, often waiting months or years for the opportunity.

The fact that an armistice has been signed between the French and the Viet Minh has altered but little the situation in Cochinchina. The main difference is that, officially, hostilities are at an end, and the Viet Minh are now pursuing a very shrewd propaganda policy directed more against the Indochinese government than against the French. Their hold on the native population increases daily, and their influence is greater than ever before.

In no sense are the chapters which follow a direct reproach to any specific person. To avoid any possible misunderstanding I have, therefore, altered the names of people, places and, in a certain measure, the chronological order of events, a liberty essential in order to observe the traditional regulation which guarantees the absolute anonymity of all men serving in the Foreign Legion. I myself enlisted under a *nom de guerre*.

HENRY AINLEY

Chapter

I

Five of us had been sent up from Saigon to replace the latest casualties. After an hour's run through paddy-fields and plantations we arrived at the Regimental HQ, a conglomeration of jerry-built huts which had been set up in the middle of what looked like a drained-out paddy-field. The whole affair was surrounded by barbed wire and ditch defences protected by armed sentries in battledress; it looked very warlike after the merry-go-round of Saigon!

Within a few minutes we were whipped through the different administrative offices and found that we were being assigned to the Nth Battalion. The latter was stationed in the village of Hoc Mon, a couple of miles away, and, since a Battalion truck happened to be there, we were told to board it and get on our way. A brief and bone-shaking run down a dusty potholed road brought us to a peaceful-looking little village in which we had a fleeting glance of palm-trees, pagodas, pigs and children, before drawing up inside the Battalion headquarter post. It was nearly midday and the place was entirely deserted as we piled off the truck with our gear beneath the blinding heat of the sun. Within a few seconds, however, we were surrounded by the old hands eager to weigh us up and exchange news.

Amongst them was Bodenko, with whom I had been through

my initial training in North Africa. After a brief welcome he
assumed the role of host and began to show me round the post
and give me the general lowdown. From twelve to three was the
official siesta time in Indochina, so there was really nothing else
to do.

We were strolling through the shacks which served as platoon
dormitories when through a window I saw two Europeans in
shorts, stripped to the waist, who were dragging an Annamite
native out of a little square brick building, set slightly apart from
the others. Their torsos were streaked with blood and running with
sweat; the man they were dragging was obviously in very bad
shape, covered with bloody weals, and from where I was I could
hear his breath coming with horrible moaning rattles. They got
him to what looked like a coalshed, opened the door, slung him
in, locked the door and sauntered off laughing and chatting as
they went. Surprised, I turned to Bodenko and asked him what it
was all about. He hardly bothered to look and in a bored sort of
way said:

'Oh, that's just Sergeant Estaing and Sergeant Frejus with a
"bounyoul"[1]. They caught him this morning out on patrol and
he's suspected of being in contact with the Viets. They've just been
"interrogating" him for Lieutenant Blairot, the Security Officer.'

Suddenly I felt very sick and shaky and I realised that the
months of training and theory in the Foreign Legion's North
African training battalions had done nothing to prepare me for the
brutal facts of everyday Indochinese life.

While we were downing some beers in the canteen my thoughts
kept coming back to the incident we had just witnessed, and I
paid little attention to Bodenko's conversation. It wasn't till
we were well into the second round that I realised what had struck
me so forcibly—Bodenko's indifference, and it hadn't been
feigned. I knew Bodenko pretty well. He was a big thick-set
Russian, about forty years old, who had deserted from the
Russian Army to the Germans in 1943 and finally found his way

[1] French Army slang for natives.

into the Foreign Legion in 1950. The intervening years he had spent wandering from DP camp to DP camp and from zone to zone. He had seen and suffered a great deal in his life but he was far from being insensitive. However it didn't seem worthwhile to broach the matter right away. Instead we started to reminisce about our early Legion days in North Africa.

In November 1950, driven by a mixture of misguided idealism and general disgust with everybody else's inertia about Communism, I had arrived at Sidi Bel Abbes intending to join the French Foreign Legion and go out to Indochina to fight the Communists. I spent twenty-four hours wandering about the town, looking at the barracks and the white-kepi'd Légionnaries, before picking up enough courage to take the plunge. When I walked up to the main gates and announced to the duty NCO that I wanted to join he was completely taken aback. At first he thought that I was pulling his leg, but after a few seconds' hesitation he put me in the hands of an orderly who led me off to the Security Adjutant.

The equivalent of a Warrant Officer in the British Army, the Adjutant was one of the Legion's special security officers and he couldn't understand why I wanted to join. I was in good health, seemingly sane, had plenty of money on me and yet I came all the way to Sidi Bel Abbes to join the Legion. Finally, after a lengthy questioning, he told me that I might be accepted if further checkups on my motives for volunteering, identity and political background proved favourable. Meanwhile, he said, I would be assigned to the Compagnie de Passage No. 3 where recruits were kept until cleared by Security. Before dismissing me he warned me that I was about to go into something which would undoubtedly surprise me but added that everybody in the Legion, himself included, had been through it and that if I took it all in good part life wouldn't be too bad. The initial shock of joining was somewhat eased however by the very unorthodoxy of my arrival.

Normally candidates for the Legion were assembled at Marseille, having already spent a few days or weeks in the recruiting centres of Paris, Lyon, or Lille, for security screening. They left Marseille in batches of from two to three hundred after a thorough vetting by the French 2ème Bureau[1] and the Legion's own highly skilled security officers, experts at weeding out such undesirables as murderers, major criminals, hopeless perverts and, above all, Communists. For the latter to infiltrate into the Legion was virtually impossible. The Foreign Legion was one of the last strongholds against Communism and was rightly and fiercely jealous of the record. Since I had joined directly at Sidi Bel Abbes, the administrative centre and the spiritual home of the Foreign Legion, my past and motives for joining had to be checked and cross-checked; it was January 1951 before I was effected to an initial training company.

The interval I had to spend at the C.P.3, a small three-storied building surrounded by a square in the heart of one of the two main barracks of Sidi Bel Abbes. Completely shut off from the outside world, my only contact with it was through the batches of fresh recruits who came in from Marseille twice weekly. They only stayed a week, however, having already accomplished the majority of the induction formalities in France—with the result that I made few, if any, friends while there. It became most depressing to be a semi-permanent spectator of others' hardships. They were chivvied and chased and hounded around, but at least they left after a week of it, while I had to stay on being used rather like a lead steer in a slaughter-house. The only thing I appreciated about the C.P.3 treatment was that it made everything that followed seem almost a pleasure and a relief.

Finally my turn came to leave. Christmas and New Year had passed by in a wave of nostalgic and alcoholic stupor and my head had just stopped spinning when I was told that I had been assigned to a training battalion in Mascara—a town in the foothills of the Atlas Mountains well known for the strength of the local wine and the toughness of the Legion's NCO instructors. My last three days were spent being rushed through the necessary formalities, being equipped with a mountain of gear, none of which fitted—

[1] Equivalent to MI 5.

the Legion was equipped with the cast-offs from the regular army and the French are very small—and drawing my first pay. Ninety days from the time I had joined at six francs a day, it came to about ten shillings. Luckily I still had some money left from the thirty-odd pounds I had on me when I joined.

As I lined up with a hundred and seventy-nine other recruits on the day of our departure for Mascara I couldn't help feeling apprehensive. I had become so used to the unpleasantness of the C.P.3 that I almost regretted it for the unknown of what lay ahead. I had heard so much barrack-room gossip about the hardships of training that I found it very difficult to console myself with the thought that it was at least a step towards getting out to Indochina which had been the object of my joining the Legion. After a pre-dawn reveille and a morning of roll-calls and checking of lists we were handed over to a bunch of tough Teutonic-looking instructors; they were the NCOs who had come down from Mascara to fetch us. The senior NCO snapped us to attention a few times, then stood us at ease and told us to listen. We were, he said, about to leave an earthly paradise which we would bitterly regret if we stepped so much as a millimetre off the beaten track and . . . that he and the other NCOs with him were going to make us Légionnaires in the space of nine weeks whether we liked it or not. We were then marched off to a line of waiting lorries. Within five minutes, after a few vigorous reprimands, we had already learned that it was best to obey rapidly and in silence. We boarded the lorries a thoroughly chastened band and left Sidi Bel Abbes unwept and unsung. Another batch of *bleus*, raw recruits, on their way into the melting pot.

In spite of the sun which was relatively hot even though it was January, I was very glad of my greatcoat as the convoy climbed up into the hills and by the time we got to Mascara late in the afternoon we were all shivering from the unaccustomed cold. Not for long, however. As soon as the trucks ground to a halt in the Mascara barrack square they were surrounded by a swarm of NCOs and corporals who yelled at us to off-load with our gear and form up in three ranks at the double. Not fast enough the first time, so the stress was laid on 'AT THE DOUBLE'. Ten minutes of chasing around with all our gear and we got the hang of it and formed up in three ranks at the double, sweating and trembling from the effort. An hour later we had been subdivided into platoons and groups and bequeathed to our respective NCO and corporal instructors. The latter chivvied us into the buildings, three stories high, built about 1840 and never touched since. Once installed, we were told how to arrange our kit according to regulations, given half an hour to do it in and then reassembled for our first meal and a welcoming speech from the Company Sergeant-Major, a fearsome individual who would have done credit to a Guards regiment. The gist of what he had to say was that we were there for nine weeks. In that time we would have to learn basic drill, combat routine, armament, regulations, French and what the Legion stood for. We would rarely have a moment to ourselves. We would be mercilessly dealt with if we broke any regulation whatsoever and we would be Légionnaires by the end of it. If not, those who failed at the passing-out exam would just have to go through a new instruction period. He said this with a dry little laugh which sent a shiver down my spine. His final warning was for blind obedience to all orders, no matter what we cared to think of them.

When I came to three weeks later I began to understand what the training was all about. Three weeks in which the majority of us were reduced to throbbing lumps of pain and fatigue-racked flesh, whose only idea was sleep. We had no time for drink, little to smoke in, and none to feel sorry for ourselves. Having reduced us to an appropriate state of receptivity, our instructors then proceeded to instil in us the finer arts of doing an about-turn, saluting, marching in step and rifle drill. The daily marches became longer and by the end of the first month, when we had our first route march, only forty per cent failed to keep up. Even the inevitable trotting around at the double whenever moving alone between two points, very nearly became a habit.

When I had my first monthly physical check-up I had lost a good fifteen pounds in weight, felt like hell, but could still keep going in spite of my 32 years which was ten years above average. By force of having dinned into my ears that I would never make a Légionnaire, I began to come up to some of the standards required and by the time the instruction period was over I passed out second of the company, and was sent off to Sidi Bel Abbes to join a corporals' training squad. The first five of us were sent, including Bodenko, who had been third.

Bodenko and I and the three others were delighted to have a crack at getting our corporal's stripes and felt very keen and confident about our futures. A state of affairs which lasted until we got to Sidi Bel Abbes and reported to the WO in charge of the training platoon we had been assigned to. He was about the toughest and least prepossessing individual I was to meet in my three years in the Legion. He greeted us by announcing that what we had gone through in basic training was child's play compared to what was waiting for us. He refused to admit failure, and by the end of four months we would either be corporals or corpses. Before dismissing us he informed us that during working hours, unless with an instructor, we were never to move except at the DOUBLE. I suddenly wished that I had gone straight out to Indochina. It was mid-March, the African summer was beginning to heat up and I had had a bellyful of galloping around back in Mascara. Corporal's stripes began to look much less inviting.

We had arrived on a Friday; by the Monday morning the other candidates had arrived from different training companies, we had been equipped, sorted out and sub-divided into groups. At eight o'clock we were told to fall in and we were presented to the WO, Adjutant Rivière, by his senior NCO, Sergeant de Hoog. We were treated to a short blood-and-thunder speech of warning about the idleness, filth and general incompetence he had already noticed in all of us and we were given till midday to rectify all that. The next three days were a repetition of everything we had

B   17

all been through in basic training but in a diabolically concentrated form. By Thursday we had scrubbed, polished, sewn and cleaned ourselves to such a point that Rivière found no more than half a dozen complaints to make about each one of the fifty of us and announced that we were just presentable enough to be taken outside the barracks to a training field about five miles away. After a fortnight of ceaseless badgering by the instructors the platoon began to look like soldiers, and the germ of a collective spirit was born. As we improved, the constant badgering eased off, though the discipline remained as severe as ever. The slightest mistake or offence meant hours of extra drill or just doubling around the square with full equipment—a pleasantry which nobody enjoyed except those watching.

Coupled with the purely physical side of the training—drill, armament, combat, fire control, etc., we were submitted to an intensive brainwashing to prove to us that the Legion was a *corps d'élite*, that the Legion replaced family, country and all our past connections, that we were in the way of becoming the élite of the Legion, etc. On top of all that there were sessions devoted to the Indochinese war, in which we were warned that few if any of the natives, even those who were pro-French, could be trusted as they were nothing but 'bounyouls'. It was the aspect of the course which impressed me the least.

I was, however, staggered by the purely military part. In spite of my totally unmilitary background and character I found that I was being turned into a fairly good soldier, outwardly at least. I say 'outwardly' because I found it hard to accept as good a discipline that was based on fear. Fear was the controlling factor throughout the Legion on all scales of the hierarchy, whether it was of prison, loss of rank or of being sent to the Legion's special disciplinary battalions. I had little time for reflection during the course. We were driven hard purposely so that if we were due to crack up we would do so before being promoted corporals.

Fortunately, at the end of April, in the middle of the course, we had a three-day break. April 30th was the traditional fête of the Foreign Legion, to celebrate a company of the Legion which had allowed itself to be massacred, with great heroism, in Mexico at the village of Cameronne on April 30th, 1862. In the course of years the fête had become the equivalent of the feasts of slaves in Roman times, and the 29th of April and 1st of May had been added in order to let the Légionnaires work up steam for and get over the ill effects of the 30th's orgy. Apart from a ceremonial parade in which we all had to take part, we had three clear days in which to do anything we liked without any fear of disciplinary measures being taken. A fact which led to inevitable heavy drinking and a subsequent settling of private feuds.

In our platoon Adjutant Rivière and Sergeant de Hoog kept well out of the way, not only so that we could let off steam freely, but also because they were quite rightly certain that we held a number of grievances against them which we wouldn't hesitate to settle, especially between dusk and dawn. As it was, most of us came out of the celebrations slightly battered and hung-over but with no really bitter feelings towards each other. Bodenko and I had a scrap with a couple of the corporals in charge of us, three of the platoon deserted and one chap got knifed, but apart from that nothing very serious happened.

The deserters were arrested a few days later and got sixty days apiece. Bodenko, the corporals and I were summoned before Rivière and told to forget all about our fight, and Schmidt, who had been knifed in the belly, pulled through after a major operation and a ten-day struggle against death. He was a great hulking brute of a German, an ex-prizefighter, whose main hobby was beating up the smaller members of the platoon and then terrorising them to such an extent that they didn't dare complain. His luck broke on the night of the 30th and one of his ex-victims knifed him. He was found sprawling in a pool of blood on the floor of the room a little before midnight and was rushed to hospital: though not before he had been able to name his assailant. A Czech named Kovic maintained that he had been acting in self-defence and after a few days in the guard-room was allowed to rejoin the

platoon and finish the course. Meanwhile, Bodenko and I were
made to realise by devious means that it had been extremely
unwise of us to fight with the Corporal Instructors, 30th of April
or no. They were both vindictive bastards and right up to the
end of the course we did a deal more than our fair share of
fatigues, extra drills and spells of guard duty. By the time the
passing-out exams came round I was ready to give up from sheer
exhaustion and had dropped another ten pounds in weight.
Bodenko was in about the same shape. The only thing that saved
us from cracking up completely were the rare occasions we managed to get a pass into town. Then, pooling our resources, we went
into Arab dives to stoke up on skewered mutton and later into
the wine shops to drown our sorrows.

When the final results were posted up I found that I had passed
out 8th, Bodenko 18th or so. But my luck was out. I was assigned
to Mascara as Corporal Instructor, while Bokenko was included
in the next reinforcement for Indochina, due to leave within a
few days. I was completely disgusted—it was mid-July, the heat
was terrible and all I could look forward to was a continuation
of the same dreary existence. When I arrived back at Mascara
I hoped that life would be easier. Instead of just being taught,
I had to do the teaching and learn that a corporal is the lowest
expression of human life. After a month of being an instructor
I learned that I was on the list of corporals to be sent back to
Sidi Bel Abbes to take a sergeant's course of four months,
after which I would be sent back to Mascara for a year as instructor
again. It was too much. By persistent badgering of the authorities
I managed to get myself included in the September reinforcement. I felt very relieved, for by then I had nine months of
pounding around barrack squares and the North African goat
tracks. My feet and my morale just couldn't have stood any more
of it.

In mid-September I was sent off to the Legion's overseas
drafting camp at Nouvion, thirty miles or so from Oran. It was
there that the reinforcement detachments were grouped for the

embarkation formalities: injections, pay and equipment. It was
stuck in a completely deserted area, near a tiny village, to cut
down on last-minute desertions. There was a curiously happy-go-
lucky atmosphere about the camp and the Legion's iron discipline
was considerably relaxed so that morale would stay high; my
own was considerably boosted by a surprise forty-eight hour
leave pass. I went down to Oran, where I stayed in a good hotel
and wallowed in the almost forgotten luxury of hot baths for
most of the two days.

When I got back to Nouvion I found that my detachment was
leaving the next day to embark on the SS *Pasteur*—a German
liner seized as war reparations and converted into a troopship.
She was the fastest and best which the French possessed, the rest
being decrepit old hulks which were of no further use to their
owners.

In true army style we were ready for the 10 p.m. departure
by 5 a.m.—the train which was to run us down to the docks took
six hours to make the thirty miles and we were all thoroughly
browned off when we off-loaded from our straw-littered cattle-
trucks the next morning. Apart from the detachment from the
Legion there were Moroccan, Algerian and a few odd groups of
French specialists waiting to embark. The hour's wait for the
Pasteur, coming from Marseille, we filled by taking advantage of
the free wine and snacks being distributed by the Red Cross and
other organisations.

Around seven in the morning she came alongside and already
seemed to be so crowded that it was hard to see where they were
going to put another two thousand of us. After what seemed an
eternity of struggling up gangways, down ladders, along corridors,
lugging my kitbag and suitcase, I finally found a space to stow
my gear and time to take my bearings. We had been allocated a
'tween-deck space in which there were sufficient benches, tables
and hammock space for about four hundred very small men.
We were nine hundred strong and rather large. An inevitable
slightly vicious free-for-all immediately began for the best places,

a state of affairs which lasted throughout the twenty-one-day trip. The eating question was solved by the shift system. Sleeping was another matter and as soon as dusk fell there was an indescribable chaos on the upper decks as Senegalese, Moroccans, Algerians, Légionnaires and French fought for hammock space with no holds barred. The officers and NCOs very wisely kept out of the way and let us settle our own differences. The heat and the crowded conditions, with about nine thousand aboard, made the trip rather nightmarish, but at least we had nothing to do except eat, drink and amuse ourselves as best we could.

We made stops at Port Said and Aden, during which I was appointed duty NCO[1] of ship's prison, in the bowels of the ship, mainly because of my English nationality and the fear that I would desert. Desertion was a frequent occurrence and the Legion took every precaution to cut down individual temptation. As it was we had four deserters, all German, while going through the Canal. I heard later that they had been caught the same day and put on the next Indochina-bound trooper.

We put in to Singapore to refuel and restore and once again I was detailed to the prison—by that time overcrowded with petty offenders, a would-be assassin and a few drunks, and the only sight I caught of it was the lights of the town as the *Pasteur* steamed out at midnight.

When we left Singapore on October 6th 1951 we had picked up a batch of officers from GHQ Saigon, who had come down to meet us with the drafting orders and the destinations for the different units aboard. The thirty-six-hour run from Singapore to Cap St Jacques, down-river from Saigon, was spent in trying to sort out the troops destined for Saigon and Cochinchina from those Tonkin-bound, where all the heavy fighting and losses were.

I was assigned to four different regiments within twenty-four hours, my fourth and supposedly final assignment being the 5th REI which was stationed in Tonkin. It was good news, as most

[1] In the Legion, Corporals count as troops, though they can be used as acting NCOs without their privileges.

of my Legion acquaintances were destined for the same outfit.

We got to Cap St Jacques at dawn and the Saigon units, about a thousand all told, began off-loading into a Liberty ship. The rest of us lined the rails of the troopship watching the inevitable bedlam down on the Liberty's decks where batmen were trying to get their officers' luggage together; a biggish group of junior officers were wondering where to put themselves; French, North African and Senegalese were squabbling over just which bit of deck belonged to whom, and a small Legion detachment settled the problem by occupying all the deck they could spread out on. I felt thankful that my turn was for later.

The sun was getting too hot for comfort, so I strolled off to find a shady corner. I had taken only a few steps when I saw a hot, harassed, paper-laden young Lieutenant bearing down and obviously intending to collar me. Sensing impending disaster of some kind I tried to dodge out of sight—but it was too late. He called me over and, asking for my name and rank, scribbled them down on one of his lists, then started to bawl me out. 'Why the hell wasn't I down on the Liberty?' He'd been looking for me all morning, etc. . . . I tried to edge in a word, to tell him that I was already assigned and that my assignment had been confirmed a short while before by a Captain G——. He didn't give a damn about Captain G——, on his list I was for Saigon, the Saigon units were a corporal short and to Saigon I could bloody well go. By now heat and flurry had got him to the pitch where discussion was useless, and so, remembering the French Army dictum 'Act first, then discuss', I went below, collected my gear and struggled aboard the Liberty—just in time; she cast off a few minutes later.

Hot, dishevelled and dispirited I squeezed through the crawling mess of men, kitbags, trunks and coils of rope trying to find the NCO in charge of the Legion detachment. It turned out that there were three separate detachments and that I wasn't listed on any of them. In despair I asked the most sympathetic-looking of the three NCOs to add me to his list as a supernumerary until we

got to the Saigon base. After a lot of palaver and beer he agreed.
Though it was only an eight-hour run up the river, the heat, the
lack of shade and the fact that there was nothing to drink but
lukewarm beer and sour wine made an endless nightmare of the
trip. The monotonous flat swampy river country added to the
general impression of desolation, heightened by the innumerable
hulks of allied cargo-vessels sunk by the Japanese and now
being dismantled for scrap by a Japanese salvage company. The
Rising Sun flag fluttered on most of the hulks.

Saigon at last. It was night, and as the ship drew into the dock
I could see hundreds of bats racing round the arc-lights, under
which a brass band was sweating out a series of marches to
welcome us: on the walls behind the band scores of lizards were
snapping up the mosquitoes missed by the bats.

Once alongside, an outrageously well-dressed and cool-looking
staff-officer started a speech, which was inaudible through the
clatter of the ship's donkey-engines; a few officers disembarked
with a lot of handshaking and saluting all round and the rest of
us began to struggle ashore as the band packed up and left.

The rest of the night was straight universal army hell—fall in,
fall out—board lorries, get off—fall in, fall out—you there,
you sleep here, the next ten over there—sheets? mosquito nets?
—in the morning—canteen?—closed. But it was Indochina
with its incomparable moon, mosquitoes, bull-frogs and cricket-
song.

After a bug-ridden night, a shower and a shave, I woke up
to the fact that I had better find out where I ought to be. A tour
round the different offices and I realised that officially I didn't
exist—except as a pencilled addition to an out-of-date list.
By a stroke of luck I ran across Captain G——, who had assigned
me to Tonkin, and told him my tale of woe—he laughed, promised to see what he could do and that was the last I ever saw or
heard of him. Three or four days of futile hunting around and
getting bawled out taught me my lesson and I adopted the
attitude prevalent throughout Indochina. It was too hot and the

heat too tiring and, anyway, why worry?—there were others there being paid for that. Since I was assigned nowhere and only provisionally attached to the roll-call list, I could do as I liked so long as I checked in at the main office twice daily.

Late in the afternoons, once the hard sweltering core of heat had eased off, I went out to have a look at Saigon. A strange city, easy to get acquainted with but hard to know. A city where everything could be bought—honour, honours, opium, Cadillacs, guns, chewing-gum, women, money, children, military secrets, rubber, life—and sold. A twin city, Saigon-Cholon was inextricably woven together; Saigon, the classic French colonial city with spacious boulevards and vast administrative buildings, tree-lined avenues and garden-surrounded villas; Cholon, a swarming ant-heap with pot-holed dirt roads and a straw-thatched shanty town, tortuous stall-lined alleys and child-infested hovels. For local colour Cholon had everything to offer—Chinese druggists, bars, brothels, delicatessens, chop-suey booths, dance halls, opium dives, bazaars—prices ran according to rank for the military. Cholon however was no place for a European alone after dusk, so I went on down to Saigon. There European-style restaurants, bars and cabarets were doing a roaring trade and on all sides the streets were crowded with officers and NCOs from the innumerable administrative centres looking for amusement or hurrying along to keep a date. In the avenues never-ending streams of jeeps, taxis, bicycles and murderous-looking *pousse-pousses*[1] tore along at breakneck speed.

But there was a tawdry, vicious, unnatural blare to all that went on in Saigon and it didn't take long to realise that the motivating forces of the ceaseless activity were the war and the piastre. The war because it poured in an unending stream of military material, of which a good percentage was diverted into normal commercial channels, and an unending stream of overpaid soldiers for the population to batten and fatten on. The piastre

[1] A modern version of the rickshaw—motor or pedal tricycles used as taxis.

because it was overvalued and a swarm of businessmen, officials, and military personnel had evolved innumerable ways and means to traffic with the exchange. Back in Paris I had read up quite a bit on the alleged piastre scandals, but had never imagined the racket to be so widespread. Everybody seemed to have a deal to settle, a man to see about a piastre or a bit of exchange business to attend to—right down to the private soldier, who could triple his pay by sending money through official channels for some local merchant.

The whole set-up was most depressing and it was with relief that I heard my name called out on the morning of October 11th. A regiment stationed in Cochinchina, some 30 miles from Saigon, was badly in need of more men and they were sending along about fifteen of us. Before leaving I was warned that my papers were still missing and that I would have to explain the matter when I got to Regimental HQ, but as I scrambled up into the lorry I couldn't have cared less—finally I was assigned. I didn't even mind that my final destination was Cochinchina, where there was only guerilla warfare and pacification duties instead of the real war that was going on up in Tonkin. For the first time I began to feel some justification in my having joined the Foreign Legion, and from what I had heard from the old hands the activity was quite intense in the south.

Chapter

2

THE TRIP TO the Regimental Headquarters was about an hour's run from Saigon on the main Saigon-Cambodia trunk road. A main road so narrow and bumpy that the truck had to slow down considerably when passing oncoming traffic. Every kilometre or so there were watch-towers, smothered in barbed wire and earthwork defences manned by scruffy-looking local militiamen.

The surrounding countryside of plantations and paddy-fields seemed very deserted. The only signs of active life I noticed were in the occasional groups of battered straw-roofed hovels which we passed from time to time. They were usually swarming with near-naked children and pigs of all sizes, with an occasional old crone squatting in a doorway with what looked like an enormous cigar between her teeth.

We got to the RHQ just before midday and, since the siesta was inviolable in Indochina, our arrival was none too well received. We were rattled through the various administrative offices, made to feel thoroughly unwelcome, and five of us were then told that we were being drafted to the Nth Battalion. I came in for particular attention because of my missing papers and I was very thankful when we were told to get on the Battalion truck which had been sent to collect us.

27

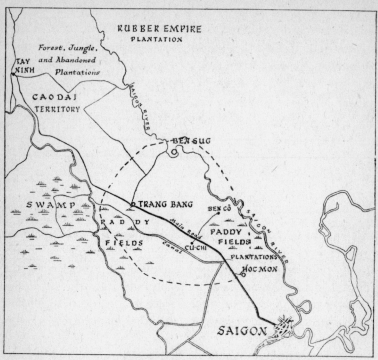

FIRST TERRITORY. (*The author's sector during this period is bounded by the dotted line.*)

After the somewhat brutal awakening at Hoc Mon, I spent the rest of the siesta with Bodenko in the canteen drinking beer and reminiscing. When three o'clock came round he went off to work and I to the Battalion offices.

The rest of the afternoon was filled up by the now all too familiar routine of offices, forms, questions, but as luck would have it neither the Battalion nor the Company Commander were there—both away on operations—and there was no question of our being definitely assigned to a platoon for another eight days. That meant eight days free, free even of guard duty. In an odd way I was very pleased to get that eight-day respite—the sight of the native leaving his interrogation had roused my curiosity and I wanted to find out more about the matter. Bodenko's indifference had convinced me that it must be of such common occurrence as to arouse little or no interest and yet it seemed scarcely credible that the French—after all they had suffered during the war—could tolerate such a practice.

Bodenko came round to my room and picked me up about six o'clock. He suggested a pub in town where we could eat and have a quiet drink and off we went. It turned out to be a pleasant enough place owned by an enormously fat Sino-Annamite woman, all chins, breast and smiles, known as La Grosse Maria.

Once through a horde of squalling children, puppies and little black piglets, we found ourselves in the single deliciously cool room of a native thatched-roof house, which was bliss after the sweltering heat of the brick-huts in the post. We ordered and ate a reasonably good dinner, and by the time we had lit our first cigarettes we had got through the small talk and caught up with the gap caused by Bodenko's earlier departure for Indochina and our respective doings during the three months we had been separated.

The moment seemed right, so I began to question him about that morning's incident. At first he was surprised that I should harp on such a trivial matter, but agreed that he had felt the same way at first and added that it was so frequent an occurrence that he had ceased to take any notice, or as little as possible: it was, he said, like the heat, the climate, the army—unpleasant enough to be worth forgetting if one wanted to live quietly and without trouble.

With that we got up, paid great fat smiling Maria and, threading our way through the puppies, piglets and Maria's progeny, strolled out into the cooling moonlit night. We never had another opportunity to get back on to our after-dinner topic again; Bodenko got blown up by a mine later—dead on the field of honour—before we could talk properly again.

The next two years were to confirm what I had sensed the

first day. Torture and brutality were routine matters in the questioning of suspects, and frequently I was obliged to be an unwilling and disgusted witness, powerless to intervene. Unfortunately brutality and bestiality were not exclusively reserved for official suspects. Rape, beating, burning, torturing of entirely harmless peasants and villagers were of common occurrence in the course of punitive patrols and operations by French troops, throughout the length and breadth of Indochina; the same measures evidently being applied to *bona fide* Vietminh as well. Nor were these measures exclusively applied by the men; officers and NCOs assumed an active and frequently dominating role.

It was not an infrequent occurrence to hear these men bragging of the number of murders or rapes they had committed or the means of torture they had applied, or the cash, jewels or possessions they had stolen. If one queried the morality of their actions the immediate reflection was: 'Well, hell, they are only "bounyouls". Who the devil cares, anyhow?' Before such a widespread and generally accepted practice there was nothing to do but look, listen and say nothing.

In the more blatant cases of aggression against peaceful natives a scapegoat was usually found to shoulder the responsibility should a native have the courage to insist that the authorities take action—but little was ever done to get to the root of the problem: a Légionnaire is rarely more than a reflection of his immediate superior and his actions are generally directly related to the attitude and worth of his superior. Moreover, he knew that official language was good at camouflage: rape, murder, torture, loot became questioned, killed in combat, interrogation of suspects, recovery of rebel material: he realised that as long as he didn't overstep the limits of tolerated banditry his actions would pass uncensured.

The Intelligence Service, or 2ème Bureau, at the post was the information service for the Battalion and the territorial area for which the Battalion was responsible. There, all the information coming in from outside sources and subsidiary units and posts was correlated. There, also, were brought in suspects and Viet prisoners for questioning before being sent on to a higher authority —if it seemed necessary and if the individual was not in too bad shape after his or her initial interrogation.

In charge was Lieutenant Blairot, responsible for the organisation as a whole and the exploitation of information received. His staff consisted of three Annamite NCO interpreters, attached to the French Army and paid as French personnel, who were responsible for the office work and the vocal side of the interrogations, and two European NCOs, of whom one was responsible for the prisoner compound, feeding and general discipline, the other for the Bande Noire.

The Bande Noire in various forms and under various appellations was an intrinsic and vital part of the different units forming the French Expeditionary Force. Recruited from Viet deserters, local thugs and fugitives from justice, the Bande Noire varied in strength but rarely in quality; the men, who were rated as auxiliaries, received a nominal pay and did very well on the side. Their loyalty was assured by the fact that nine-tenths of them were being actively sought for either by the Viets or by the local police and often had stiff prices on their heads.

Once in the Bande Noire, however, they were untouchable, well-armed, lodged and free. The name of Bande Noire was widely used for these groups on account of the black cotton shirts and trousers they wore so as not to be seen at night, the major part of their activities taking place between dusk and dawn —and a good name it was. The sight of a platoon of those tough, grim-faced, cold-eyed killers slipping out of the village at night inevitably conjured up visions of dark and midnight deeds.

Their official designation, however, was that of special security agents and their job was to get information about Viet movements, plans and positions—and it was the results that counted. Daytimes they skulked around the neighbouring villages and markets, getting into contact with the people, listening and

Suspects in for questioning

following those they knew to be strangers. Each man would have his own speciality and district—some even managed to filter their way through to the Viets and to stay with them for a few days. At night they would go out to ambush reported Viet supply convoys or else round up peasants and tradesmen suspected of being in league with the Vietminh; these last would be brought back for questioning.

Frequently, if they considered it unnecessary or tedious to bring a man in, he would be quietly knifed or strangled, and later, if the body were found, the murder would be put down to Viet terroristic activity. Inevitably the cash and portable values of any household suspected and raided passed into their possession.

Universally feared and hated by the local population on

32

account of their thieving, blackmailing, racketeering propensities, the Bande Noire did have one redeeming feature, and that was their courage in combat. It was unknown for one of them to be taken prisoner alive—they knew too well what was waiting for them if ever the Viets could get them. For it was they who were usually instrumental in the application of the torture or beatings employed during the interrogation of Viet suspects, and on patrol or in ambush they seldom left any wounded alive or took any wounded prisoner. Autonomous, they lived apart from the rest of the post with the women they had married or stolen; feared and hated by the people, they rarely went out less than three at a time: indomitable fighters, they were respected by the Europeans, and they were of vital importance for the information which they brought in. It was rare that a man left the Bande Noire till he was killed or died of wounds, for there was nowhere left in Indochina for him where he would be safe from the inevitable retribution, either from the Vietminh or the Vietnam.[1]

In charge of the Battalion's Bande Noire was big, fat, pleasant-faced Sergeant Estaing; rosy-cheeked and smiling, he looked like a poster for 'Beer is best'. His job was to control the men and regulate their daytime activities, while at night he led them and indicated the job in hand. A cool, efficient killer, he had been with the LVF, the Légion des Volontaires Français, French Volunteers in the German Army, in the Russian campaign and later had been able to swing himself into a Savoyard maquis outfit. His outlook was very simple and very sane: shoot first and ask afterwards. In over ten years of uninterrupted fighting —Russia, Germany, France, Indochina—he had managed to come through without a single serious wound. Adored by his men, whom he controlled with an iron fist, he was scrupulous in all that concerned the takings of the Bande Noire where loot was pooled, sold and the results divided on a share basis,

[1] The Vietminh were and are Communist Indochinese. The Vietnam were and are Baodai or French Indochinese.

his own being slightly higher than the rest. His skill and coolness in combat had earned for him six Croix de Guerre and the Military Medal as well as an amnesty for wartime deeds against the French government. Incidentally his decorations were all won the hard way.

The normal procedure when the Bande Noire brought in suspects was stereotyped. The men came in from a night patrol or ambush tired, dirty and famished—with them a man even more so, since he had usually been walking for miles through scrub and paddy-fields with his hands tied behind his back and obliged to keep up with his captors, under the threat of a cut throat or a bullet in the back. As soon as they arrived at the Post, Estaing reported to Lieutenant Blairot that he had brought in a suspect for questioning, gave a summary of the night's activity and took his men off to rest.

The suspect would be left in Blairot's office squatting on the floor with his hands still tied. After an hour or two, with the office staff of Annamite interpreters going about their routine occupations, the suspect would be suddenly thrown on to his back by a kick from Blairot, who would go on to give the man a vociferous harangue in French, of which he understood not a word. Then two ex-Viet specialists would start a systematic softening-up which consisted of a kidney and liver massage with rubber hose and feet—army boots *de rigueur*.

Jerked back into a squatting position, the man was left alone for a few seconds while his bowels automatically emptied—then a rapid shower of questions and cross-questions on identity, job, domicile, friends and military employ if any. If, from the questions posed by Blairot through an interpreter, it turned out that the man was innocent he was sent off to the prisoner compound to recover and spend six months working for the army free (the price of being a suspect), and was graciously allowed a weekly visit from his family once the latter received notification of his detention. If, however, he could or would not clarify his situation, over he went again for another massage—back into a squatting position—re-questioning by Blairot, who, to aug-ment the importance of the affair, would begin a steady rhythmic backhand-forehand beating of the man's throat and neck with a metal ruler. By that time evidently the man would be incapable of speech, and mad with rage Blairot would kick him back on to the floor, order another kidney-liver massage and have the man dragged out of his office as soon as he had fainted. Blairot had several decorations and was waiting for the Legion of Honour for 'Services rendered', which would help his promotion.

Once a prisoner or suspect had proved resistant to such rela-tively humane methods, and it was frequently the case, Sergeant Estaing and Sergeant Frejus, who was responsible for the prisoner compound, were called in to take over and apply the special treatment—which was too tiring for Blairot to do more than watch.

Beforehand, the two ex-Viet Bande Noire specialists had invariably warned the victim of what to expect, then dragged him off to the little brick house in the middle of the other build-ings. Once there, Estaing and Frejus would rip off the man's clothes and set to with split-canes, rubber hose and fists. When they got tired they attached electrical leads to his genitals and turned on the current and, as soon as they had got back their breath, split-canes, rubber-hose and fists again. The same rhythm would be kept up until the prisoner was either dead or too far gone to react.

He would, if still alive, be hauled off to the special cell where he was left for a day, two days, three days without food or water and then treatment as before.

Basically the only person to get any pleasure out of all that was Blairot. The rest, the interpreters, the Bande Noire, Estaing and Frejus, killed and tortured coldly, cleanly and without emotion—they had their job to do and they did it efficiently. Their reaction to Blairot was one of profound mistrust and contempt: the mistrust and contempt of a working

35

farmer for the week-end city amateur who comes down to his model farm to enthuse about the beauty of nature and declaim against the backwardness of the old-fashioned methods of the professional. They knew that men capable of withstanding the special treatment would never talk.

Chapter

3

A MOST UNSAVOURY side issue to the prisoner interrogation question was the attitude of the other Europeans. The majority regarded the whole matter as a necessary and inevitable evil and echoed Bodenko's outlook—a strongish minority, however, found it to be a first-class pastime, and when they had nothing better to do would gang up outside Blairot's office or the little brick house and relay to each other the latest developments. The longer and bloodier the session, the happier they were.

Fortunately for me, my eight days respite from work was over before I lost control of myself and I was obliged to concentrate on other matters than the sufferings of the few through the might of the many. The Battalion Commander and the Headquarter Company Commander had come back from operations and we 'new boys' were warned to tart ourselves up and be ready for the interview the next day, October 20th—an interview of vital importance for us as it would decide the future of our two-year stay in Indochina.

An hour's wait, mercifully short by army standards, and I found myself being summoned into the holy of holies feeling very much like a schoolboy being summoned in to see the headmaster of his school for the first time. Major Angeli, however,

A tough, chunky little man

put me at ease right away: a tough, chunky little man with
greying close-cropped hair and humorous eyes, he was nobody's
fool. After a brief summary concerning my age, rank, nationality,
former profession and military experiences—the latter made
him chuckle when I admitted to being ex-Royal Navy—he
told me that I was mature enough to realise that wading through

38

paddy-fields, falling into bamboo-spiked pits and firing shots into the air looked good on the newsreels, *n'est-ce pas*, but that he was appointing me to Headquarters as his secretary for a probationary period of three months. He then asked me if I had any request to make. I said 'No', but added that my papers had all been mislaid owing to a muddle at Cap St Jacques and that neither Saigon nor RHQ knew a thing about them or myself. 'Odd,' said he. 'They've been on my desk for two weeks.' He gave me a shake of the hand and there I was launched on a career in French Army bureaucracy—a man who was just capable of realising where overdrafts came in bank statements because they were written in red.

The job of Battalion Commander's secretary automatically implied assignment to the Headquarter Company (CCB, or Compagnie de Commandement du Bataillon), so once more I threw myself into the merry-go-round of offices to finish with the incorporation routine and to collect clothes, armament, ammunition, etc., but this time everything went much faster and I was soon through with it all, topping off the works with a brief pep-talk and 'glad to have you with us' speech from Lieutenant Baudoin, CO of the CCB.

By the time I was finished with all that it was well past five in the afternoon and I realised that I had better go and present myself to my immediate boss, Sergeant Tranchant—an ex-Vichy *fonctionnaire*—whose job was that of temporary-acting-unpaid Battalion Sergeant-Major and whom I was to succeed within a few months. Tranchant, a pale, weedy, myopic little man in his late thirties, was delighted to have me added to his staff of three, and rapidly pooh-poohed my protestations of complete ignorance of the elephantine workings of Army Administration. I could read, write and speak French? That was enough. He had two out of his three men who could either read or write or speak French, but only himself and one other who could do all three—as for the rest, he would soon set me to rights. He then rapidly introduced me to the three others and, looking at his watch, announced that it was time to knock off for the day as I had offered to stand a drink all round to celebrate my arrival in their midst. I gathered that it was an old and well-established custom to help make the newcomer feel at home and, in a strange way, it was rather warming to feel a part of *something* after so many days waiting to get settled.

The routine of settling down to a new job, getting used to the work and the new faces and participating actively in the life of the Company and the Battalion kept me very busy for the next few weeks. On top of the fact that one had to become acclimatised to the country, it was essential to get used to the change in rhythm inside the army itself. Discipline was much laxer and the rigid barrier between ranks, which had simplified matters in Africa, gave way to a much freer relationship; at first sight a pleasant though sometimes startling change which took time to get accustomed to.

Apart from the secretarial duties I was expected to fill, I found that I was on tap for escort duties, patrols and a whole variety of outside jobs whenever the Company needed a spare non-com.—the shortage of the latter being drastic. Two or three days after my debut in the Company I was sent for and asked if I wanted to go out on a patrol with the intervention platoon; a group chief was needed to replace a sergeant wounded the day before. A pleasant formula—one was always asked to participate with another formation—and psychologically sound as one could always feel that a refusal could have been made though it never was.

I changed into combat dress, buckled on my ammunition belt and grenades, got my gun and went off to the intervention section buildings to present myself to the platoon commander, Sergeant Thyme—an Armenian—trying to hide my nervousness and appear as battle-hardened as the best of them. I was still green enough to have visions of boas, tigers and Viets scattered through the brush in equal quantities and all equally lethal.

Thyme was a tough, sun-blackened, medal-bestrewn little

man who was shrewd enough to have come through four and a half years of Indochinese guerilla without a wound. After I had presented myself he slapped me on the back, told me to relax and outlined the day's programme. He was taking the platoon out on a patrol through a nearby jungle swamp where the Viets were suspected of having a hideout—my job was to cover the rear of the platoon with my group staying about 50 yards behind in open country and closing up in the thick brush. When he realised that it was my first time out he added a warning against the covered bamboo-spiked pits which abounded in the region and took me over to the group I was in charge of.

I found one or two faces I knew, from having seen them in the canteen, and by the time I had checked on the ammunition and found out the names and jobs of the ten men who formed the group it was time to set off. As we left the post in single file I felt horribly conscious of the fact that it was my first sortie and would have given anything to have said 'No' when I had been asked to go along.

Fortunately we had an hour's march along primitive tracks before we reached the area to be searched, and the new sights and sounds, the increasing heat, which I was glad to realise I supported as well as the others, and the inevitable camaraderie engendered by that type of sport all combined to get rid of the tension and make me feel at home in the platoon and with my group.

As we neared the objective Thyme signalled to the groups to spread out and we took up our planned formation advancing cautiously and in complete silence. Progress through the tangled undergrowth and wild bamboo thickets was slow and arduous and rendered doubly unpleasant by the heat and the hordes of red bush ants whose bites resembled red-hot needles. Keeping my group in cross formation, I sweated and struggled along after the others, still feeling far more scared of the wild life than of the Viets. I hadn't dared ask anyone if tigers and boas existed outside the novels I had read about Cochinchina. An eternity later we broke into a series of clearings with a few scattered cainhas, native grass-roofed huts, surrounded by manioc and groundnut plantations. Thyme signalled for the group chiefs to join him and when the three of us had arrived told us to take our groups and search the cainhas and to bring in any men we found for questioning. As I turned to go he added that he would come along with my group to show me how the job should be done; the others laughed and set off. I didn't get the laugh at first—it was friendly, but . . .

We got to our group of cainhas and left the Bren-gunner and a couple of other men on guard while Thyme, the rest and myself set to work to search. The first three were empty and there was nothing in them apart from a few bits of miserable furniture and odd pots and pans. In the fourth, however, there was a huddled group of seven or eight women and children. Thyme questioned them in Annamite and from what I could gather they knew nothing, and further questioning produced no results. Seeing that he would get nothing out of them, Thyme called them over to him one by one and searched them, taking what little money and odd bits of jewellery they had. The last to come was a girl of about sixteen, who had been trying to hide in a corner; as she reached Thyme he stretched out his hand and with a violent downward wrench ripped open her jacket and tore down her trousers, then, pulling her to him, began to fumble with her breasts and buttocks while he ripped off her earrings. Pain and fear made her set off with a series of ear-piercing shrieks which had the effect of snapping me out of the shocked inertia produced by his methods of questioning and I suddenly remembered the odd laugh of the other group chiefs. Without thinking, I grabbed him by the shoulder, pulled him off the girl and told him that he couldn't do that.

I don't know which of the two of us was the most surprised by my outburst. Still under the influence of Africa, I realised that I had laid hands on a superior and the consequence could be terrible. Thyme was so amazed that he finally burst out laughing and in the friendliest way told me that I would soon get used to a little friendly rape. To my relief the girl had taken the opportunity to bolt off into the bush with torn clothes clasped to her. In a cowardly way I was most relieved. I didn't feel up to fighting a whole army on the question of well-established traditional sports.

Luckily for me Thyme considered the incident closed, and as we came out of the hut he told the men to set fire to the cainhas. Once again I was shocked, but managed to hide the fact, and as I looked around I saw columns of smoke and clouds of sparks shooting up into the air in the direction of the other groups, who undoubtedly had been about their business in much the same way as Thyme. Meanwhile the men outside the cainhas had not been idle: as they came back from the firing of the huts I noticed that most had a chicken or two dangling from their belts and two were struggling with a piglet. That same night I downed a few of my scruples along with fried chicken and pork chops, which the men in the group had invited me to share with them. At the same time they told me that the looting question in the group worked out on a share system and they usually divided up the spoils after each sortie.

After a brief rest Thyme reassembled the platoon and we headed back the way we had come, keeping the same formation. The ants and the heat were still as fiery as before and I had all my time cut out keeping in contact with groups ahead when the visibility dropped to the end of one's nose. For some reason bits of the refrain from 'Ole man river', such as 'sweat and strain, body all troubled and racked with pain', kept humming through my head until suddenly I felt the ground give way under one foot. Luckily I had just started to put my foot down and had time to jump back and see that I had nearly walked into a Viet bamboo trap. It looked so like the tiger traps one sees in jungle films that I forgot the heat, the ants and 'Ole man river' and began to think again of all the tigers and boas I had read about. We passed a number of other traps that the others had uncovered, which helped to keep all thoughts about the Viet out of my mind.

After a time we began to progress through slightly clearer country and finally sighted the track that led back to the post and the other groups sitting in the shade waiting for us.

We were about twenty yards from them when Thyme shouted to me that there were a couple of traps ahead. I turned to warn the group and went on, the men falling into Indian file behind me. I skirted the traps and told the man behind to be careful—the word passed on down the line. Just as I broke on to the track I heard a shout from behind. I went back to see what had happened and found that the last man in the file had managed to fall into the trap and had his knee joint pierced through by a bamboo spike. It took us quite a while to get him out without causing him too much pain, and by the time we had put him on an emergency stretcher and bandaged his knee with a field dressing, it was time to get moving if we wanted to reach the post before dark.

I felt a bit awkward about the incident. It was my first time out and it would have to be in my group that a man fell into an open trap in broad daylight. A whole platoon had managed to pass it successfully, until that particular idiot managed to wander into it. On the way back I asked Thyme if I would have to make a report, and if so, what angle to take. He told me not to worry, he would say that the man had been lead scout and had fallen in while ahead of the platoon which would mean a decoration for him. In fact, some months later, after coming out of hospital with a pronounced limp for life, he was awarded the Croix de Guerre. In general practice, every man wounded when on combat escort or commanded duty was automatically awarded this decoration—loss of limb or life usually meant the award of the Médaille Militaire as well.

By the time that I had showered and eaten and downed several beers in a futile effort to drown the accumulated thirst of the day, I was so tired that the only thing I could do was to collapse into bed and go to sleep—mosquitoes, heat and ant-bites were unable to keep me awake.

My awakening was remarkably unpleasant. A boa-constrictor had me by the shoulder and was shaking me hard while a tiger kept on repeating in a monotonous growl, 'Wake up.' After what seemed an endless time I managed to get my eyes open and the local fauna fused into the person of Bodenko, who was trying to get me to wake up. I shot up with a start and realised that it was still night and that something must be radically wrong. Suddenly wide-awake, I was out of bed and into my trousers.

It appeared that the small post of Son Cat, a few kilometres away, had been attacked, was in flames and had undoubtedly been taken, as their radio didn't answer any more. The next post didn't dare send anyone as they had barely enough men to defend their own post and we had been ordered to go and find out what was going on. By scrounging through the CCB (Compagnie de Commandement du Bataillon) they had managed to rake up a platoon. I had been designated as a group leader, Bodenko was in the same group and begged me for the love of Christ to hurry as we were due to leave in two minutes. I bolted into my clothes, grabbed my gun and cartridge belt and dashed out to find my group. Three minutes later we were under way— an armoured car leading the procession followed by a GMC (a six-wheeled truck from American surplus war-stock), with two groups, the ambulance and, bringing up the rear, a Dodge 6 x 6 with my group.

As we jolted and crawled along the track through the dust and potholes I pulled myself together and rapidly found out what really had happened. Heavy firing of machine-guns, rifles and grenades had started about three o'clock in the direction of Son Cat. It had been impossible to get into radio contact with the post of Tan Muong, held by A Company, who had been unable to send a relief column as the majority of their men were away on a large-scale operation and the post would have been left wide open to an attack if they had sent anyone. A native auxiliary from Son Cat had managed to escape from the post and make his way to A Company, where he had arrived about four-thirty and reported that Son Cat had been overwhelmed by some five hundred Viets who had infiltrated into the post and set fire to the buildings. A Company had radioed through to head-quarters and there we were on our way.

After a twenty-minute run along the track we arrived at Tan Muong and the A Company post. The lieutenant in charge sent us off in direction of Son Cat preceded by a mine-detecting patrol. We had only about fifteen hundred yards to go, but fear of ambush and mines cut our speed right down. The patrol lifted two mines before we got to Son Cat. It was a small post in the middle of a rubber plantation and we didn't see it until we were on it, or what was left of it. Fortunately the Viet had gone, but before going had fired the majority of the buildings, the native huts and the main watch-tower.

The first rapid survey made, we found that the NCO and the two Légionnaires, who had been in command of the native auxiliaries, were dead and had been beheaded by machetes, a dozen of the auxiliaries dead and a score wounded, ten of them seriously. Several of the auxiliaries womenfolk had been scalped or ripped open or both, and three were dead, as well as two small children. The majority of the wounded and dead had been killed or wounded by machetes and not by bullets. One of the women who had been ripped open was pregnant; she was not dead, and in her arms she held a small child half of whose scalp was missing.

We set to work tending the wounded, putting out the fires and checking on what armament was missing. The latter was easy enough; virtually all the armament and ammunition as well as the radio set and generator had disappeared, and all the official documents of the post.

By half-past seven we had evacuated most of the seriously wounded, loaded the dead on to the GMC and found out how and why the post has been taken. It had been a perfect job and typical of the infinite pains the Viet took, and against which the only counter was ceaseless vigilance and strict application of the rules and regulations for security constantly stressed by GHQ, but unfortunately and invariably either ignored as 'stupid' or forgotten as 'useless'.

The post was manned by an NCO and two Légionnaires, who were in charge of thirty-odd native auxiliaries—their job was to protect the plantation workers during the day and by night to guard the post and the plantation buildings. The post consisted of a main defence or watch-tower, hangars and out-houses for the rubber and a medley of huts where lived the plantation coolies, the auxiliaries and their families and livestock. The whole was surrounded by a classic defence system of barbed wire, bamboo stakes and earthworks laid out in depth, with as sole entry a gate in *cheval de frise* which was closed at sundown. The original NCO in charge had applied for leave a few weeks before and had fifteen days accorded, to be taken as soon as a suitable relief was found. His men and the plantation coolies as well as all their womenfolk knew that he was leaving and the Viet had picked up the information.

Three days before, Lieutenant X, temporarily in charge of A Company, sent along Corporal Campari to take over—he was fresh from North Africa and had little more than a month's service in Indochina. After two days, in which he familiarised himself with the standing orders and general responsibilities, Campari took over officially for the duration of the other's leave. The same night the Viets struck and took the post, destroyed it and decamped with all they could lay hands on.

Throughout Cochinchina, the Vietminh had organised groups of regional troops. Recruited in the main from the local peasantry, the groups stayed in their home areas, their job being to provide transport for the regular Viet units, organise and sustain local guerilla activity, spread Viet propaganda and generally make life insecure for the French and the pro-Bao Dai natives. The regional troops also supplied the regulars with information about the French posts and troop movements and supported the regulars in action.

47

Local agents aware of the impending relief had carefully studied the layout and general disposition of the post as well as the varying degrees of loyalty of the native auxiliaries. They had outlined a plan and called in the head of a regional battalion to fix details and had then sat back and waited for the relief to take place. Between times they had found an auxiliary with a grouch and predisposed in their favour. On the night of the attack his job was to open the *cheval de frise* and let a group of Viets penetrate into the post. Once they were inside his job was finished and he could leave with his family. It all went off like clockwork. Campari made his first round about ten o'clock. As soon as he had passed, the gate was opened and the first group of Viet came in, went round the different sentinels, disposed of them and took their places. When Campari made his second round everything was in place and seemingly normal. When he asked the sentries if all was well in 'pidgin' the answer was invariably 'Yes'; he knew neither his men nor the language well enough to distinguish the least anomaly in the dark. Between Campari's rounds small groups of Viet continued to infiltrate until the post was completely surrounded from the interior as well as from the exterior.

Meanwhile other Viet units were stringing out along the road leading to Tan Muong and A Company, preparing to ambush a possible relief column and laying mines. By three o'clock everything was in place and set and as yet no one in the post had noticed a thing. The signal was given and under a covering fire from outside the Viets inside the post stormed the buildings and within a very short while had mastered the post. After a bout of vicious house-to-house and hand-to-hand fighting they had finished off the few auxiliaries still willing to offer, or capable of offering, resistance—the Europeans had been killed in the few first seconds of the action. As soon as they had gathered up the arms, ammunition and radio and generator they set fire to the buildings and left under a heavy covering fire from the outside.

Once back at Battalion HQ I washed and changed and went to the office feeling bitter and disgusted. Tranchant was waiting for me, a sly smile on his face and a bunch of papers in his hand. It was my morning's work—citations for the heroic defenders of Son Cat who had died gloriously for France in the face of over-whelming rebel forces and another for Lieutenant X for the invaluable support he had tried to bring them. It was too much for the same morning.

I went over to the canteen for a beer.

Chapter
4

I WAS THANKFUL for the routine work of my new job and other service commitments which filled the following days and weeks and left but little time or energy for worrying about personal viewpoints and ideals. First of all I had to learn the official language of French Army bureaucracy and I was constantly in trouble—writing the Major's official correspondence to superiors treating them as subordinates and to subordinates as superiors and generally lousing up the laws and edicts which had been functioning since Napoleon's day. Luckily both Tranchant and Angeli were patient if not polite and I learnt fast.

My work in the main consisted of writing up proposals for decorations, dealing with the Major's correspondence on supra-battalion level, typing orders of the day, copying high-level orders for circulation and coping with the correspondence relative to purely territorial administration—discipline, effective, transport, promotion, instruction, etc.

The office hours didn't seem too fierce at first, though I was soon to find out that they were quite long enough. The mornings ran from eight till twelve, a three-hour break for the siesta and the afternoon from three to six. The siesta was an absolute necessity on account of the heat. In the middle of the day it was virtually impossible to touch a sheet of paper without reducing it to a soggy pulp, and a man's brain just stopped ticking over.

Apart from, and on top of, purely office hours we were called on frequently to take part in parades and guards of honour at Saigon for the benefit of various visiting marshals, generals and statesmen of different nationalities. When that occurred we just had to catch up lost time by working through the night, that type of little jaunt usually taking up at least six hours. One night in three I was responsible for the guard of the Intendance depot, which was stuck on the outside limits of the village, with a group of Cambodians under my orders. The French recruited auxiliary troops in all the states of Indochina. Volunteers, they were usually stationed fairly near their countries of origin. The Cambodians were widely used in Cochinchina. The other nights I was alternatively in charge of the emergency escort group which escorted the ambulance to pick up the wounded in outlying posts and then on down to Saigon if they were in bad shape; that meant another night lost at least once a week, and also an intervention group in case of local trouble, which usually meant a good night's sleep.

With Tranchant's approval I soon worked out a schedule for my routine work and we came to a mutual agreement that as long as I kept abreast or ahead of it I could take office and spare time off to get to know the other Companies. I went off as escort with munitions and supplies, or jeeped out to Angeli (who was nearly always away on operations) for a couple of days with the official mail. I soon got to know the different posts, units and faces, and not only got the hang of the local topography but also a pretty good idea of the multiple efforts the Battalion was called upon to furnish. In Cochinchina the main tasks of the French and the Foreign Legion were to keep the roads and rivers open, the rubber plantations working, to guard bridges and factories and the implantation of new posts in areas where the Viet was dominant. The Viet activity consisted mainly in the mining of roads, attacking convoys, ambushing patrols and attacking small posts at night. Their daytime activity was slight, but they kept up sufficient activity to render normal life impossible for the French. In the villages where there were military posts circulation was safe though individual movement outside the villages was suicidal. All roads had to be opened by mine-detectors and armoured patrols daily. At night military vehicles had to be strongly escorted and all civilian traffic was forbidden. The local population, though officially friendly, had suffered from years of pacification and their friendliness was tinged by a passive resistance to French demands and a passive acquiescence to Viet requests.

All in all it was a very tiring existence, but made bearable by the very multiplicity of the extra-curricular jobs and the absolute sanctity of Sundays off, unless some major catastrophe occurred or unless I had to take the guard.

The Battalion itself consisted of five companies of Légionnaires, four field companies and the CCB—four commandos. Each field company had attached to it a commando of Cambodian or Annamite auxiliaries commanded by a core of five to eight NCOs and Légionnaires—a company of auxiliaries, attached to the Battalion and under European command, was responsible for manning the watch-towers which were dotted along the roads of the sector at regular intervals.

The Bande Noire was officially attached to the CCB, though in effect it was completely autonomous. Territorially the Battalion was responsible for a sector of about six hundred square miles within which the field companies and commandos were placed at strategic points usually in a village or at a cross-roads. Each held a post and was charged with the general security within its individual sub-sector and above all with the security and maintenance of the roads and tracks which, apart from a feeble radio network, were the only rational means of communication and liaison and which were the constant objective of local Viet sabotage.

The companies and commandos were, however, reduced to a strict security minimum of manpower, the remaining effective having been siphoned off to form a reduced combat battalion

The Bande Noire was autonomous

which was trying to oust a Viet stronghold from an outlying corner of the sector, and at the same time build a post for later control of the area. The job took over nine months to accomplish with heavy casualties; eighteen months later the Viets retook the post.

The difficulties of communication were infernal, and frequently it took days to get through the simplest kind of routine office work. The general result was that the administrative services lived and worked in a state of mild but constant confusion which, though at times maddening, cut both ways. When a high-level blast came through for non-completion of given work within a given time, we could always plead that documents or people had been inadvertently delayed at company level through lack of communication facilities.

Most mornings I got up around six, shaved, showered and went down the local market for breakfast. It was by far the best part of the day, dawn in the offing, comparatively cool, and, above all, the flies were still asleep. The market at that hour was a vociferous, multicoloured, pleasantly odoriferous bedlam lit by primitive oil flares and lamps. Peasants crowded in from outlying farms loaded down by the inevitable and traditional yoke-balanced baskets full of vegetables, fruits, chickens, eggs, fish, pigs, and sometimes even children. Lining the pavements were scores of booths and stalls selling different kinds of chop-sueys, meatballs, ricecakes, meat soups, dumplings and fruits. For sixpence one could get enough chop-suey to keep a man going till midday, and for a penny a cup of sweet coffee strong enough to wake a corpse. Breakfast in the market was an institution for most of us, and each had a favourite booth or stall. Mine was run by a little shrivelled-up one-eyed old witch who delivered long monologues at me: I never could figure out if she was being pleasant or just plain hating me, but her food was good.

Breakfast over, I went back to the post to pick up a prisoner from the compound and would take him along to clean up my room, shoes, etc. I nearly always managed to get the same one—

a pleasant middle-aged peasant from thereabouts who spoke a little French and smoked all my cigarettes. I gathered that he had been picked up as a suspect one morning. He was working in his paddy-fields, which bordered a road, when a passing military truck blew up on a mine; no one had been wounded, but, as he put it, he should have known better than not to have known that a mine was there that day. He'd been held for eight months but hoped to be let out for Christmas; married and with five children, he had an unmarried brother looking after things during his absence. By the time he'd finished my room and his daily chat it was time to get to the office and work.

At eight the sun was already uncomfortably hot and we worked and stewed until midday with occasional breaks for beer if it had arrived from Saigon—even though beer was fatal; a pint drunk meant a quart to sweat out.

Once through with lunch, for which I rarely had any appetite, though it would undoubtedly have been excellent nourishment for a polar expedition, I went off to bed feeling like a pole-axed ox, in a vain search for a little shelter and respite from the heat and the flies. By two I would be awake after a fitful snooze and, feeling terrible, shower, dress and get to the office by three to struggle through the rest of the afternoon trying to look as though I was working, and hoping like hell that there would be no rush job or emergency. Basically all the work of the day got done in the morning or late at night, the afternoon output being so full of errors that most of it had to be redone the following day.

By the time six o'clock came round I was ready to go out into the village, if it was not my turn for some night duty. In town I had unearthed a pub, run by two Annamite brothers, where the coffee was good and where I rarely saw a European. It was heaven just sitting there in the comparative cool, smoking, sipping coffee and not only thinking nothing but hearing nothing. The canteen was usually quite impossible, crowded and noisy; and inevitably one drank too much beer and spirits. In that climate it was plain suicide to drink too much of either until one became acclimatised. Afterwards it became a means of staying alive in spite of the climate—but that took time. Overall casualties from alcoholic excess allied to heat were roughly equal to the total of combat casualties.

In the course of my work I came across innumerable reports, requests and memoranda from the District Commissioner, a Frenchman by the name of Potin, and was fortunate enough in November to meet him. From the style and tone of his communications he seemed to be quite somebody. He was nearly always writing to complain that such-and-such a unit had been cattle-raiding, looting or taking prisoners in a pacified zone and demanding immediate retribution.

He was responsible for the civil administration and development of the province for a part of which the Battalion was militarily in charge. His job was to try to encourage the settlement, agriculture, cattle-raising and forestry in pacified zones, to supervise the application of law and order and to act as a buffer between the local authorities and the army when either had any reclamations to make. The army was there to oust the Viet, protect the roads and pacify local pockets of resistance, and not infrequently overstepped the line between pacified and non-pacified zones. It was accepted army practice to make off with everything movable and saleable that was found in the course of patrols and operations in the non-pacified zones, but individual *razzia*, by local commanders of small units who were short of cash, were frequent and unofficially winked at.

Potin, however, was a man of integrity and had charm and great personal courage. Devoted to his work, he toured his province incessantly by jeep with a small escort, continually seeking ways and means by which he could hasten and consolidate the security of his area: being shot at, ambushed or having attempts made on his life with grenades and mines by the Viet disturbed him not one bit.

Through his unflagging efforts to win the people over to the

French, to convince them that they would be protected against all forms of aggression, that their cattle and produce would be bought and paid for, he had managed to resurrect important agricultural districts which had for years been abandoned to skirmishing French and Viet patrols. As a result he regarded any encroachment by the army, which threatened the security of his pacified zones, as an unpardonable and intolerable act against the welfare of the colony as a whole.

An important man, his incessant stream of complaints and reports succeeded in curbing the more flagrant forays into his rebuilt areas—but it was a bitter and constant struggle in which the inevitable victim was the peasant: pacified and looted by the French, imposed upon by the Viet. Encouraged to re-settle, the peasant, once re-settled, lived in constant terror of every passing French patrol, in case it meant being re-looted; of every passing Viet patrol in case it meant a demand for rice or, worse, the placing of a mine or two near his place.

But, for all the paper war between Potin and the battalion, he was well liked by everybody. Heedless of military hierarchy, he had friends at all levels and never bothered to hide his way of thinking. Moreover, he never held any personal animosity against an NCO or junior officer who had indulged in a particularly high-handed cattle raid or looting party to raise funds—he knew too well that they were covered and unofficially encouraged from higher up and he rarely pressed for individual punishment, even in the most flagrant cases. Unfortunately for the locals, his tour of duty was ending, but before leaving in May 1952 he had the satisfaction of knowing that all his efforts had not been in vain. Just before his departure a high-level order of the day came through to the effect that in future severe disciplinary measures would be taken, regardless of rank, for any abuse of property outside official war-zones—a slender victory.

Another side of my territorial paper work brought me into contact with various Annamite property-owners who held farms, small plantations or forestry concessions in the sector and who needed military approval for the reopening or protection of their concessions.

At first I made the official blunder of treating them like human beings. Tranchant soon put me right, however—all natives were bounyouls, no matter who they were—'Never be in a hurry to help them, ignore them as much as possible, and remember that they are nothing but a bunch of bastards, anyhow'—which seemed to be a standard reaction throughout the army. It was a bit hard to understand at first, since virtually all the officers and NCOs, as well as a large percentage of the men, had native wives or congaies who were treated with a certain amount of respect —even though the majority of the women came out of a military brothel or some Saigon dance-hall.

The congaie formed an integral part of military life out there. Whenever a unit changed sector, with it went not only the official brothel but also the chattering swarm of congaies with their mothers, sisters, cousins, children and the whole lot. Often an official order came through that the congaies were forbidden, that a unit leaving an area should leave the local fauna behind and so one; on arrival the men would find the congaies waiting for them, already installed in shacks and rented rooms, and life went on as before.

The hierarchy amongst the congaies was rigid and easy to follow, their importance being based on their incomes and, since the tariff was in strict proportion to the rank of the husband, the congaie automatically assumed his rank. A comic note crept in when a man left for France. The captain commanding B company left, and Mrs Captain, having had her cry and stayed out of sight for a day or two for decency's sake, started with delicate eagerness to hunt for a new man—the captain's successor had brought along a congaie of his own and had no use for his predecessor's grass widow. After a few days of useless search and snubbing of the lecherous common soldier she wound up by making the best of a bad job and went back to work in the brothel. There amongst her colleagues she was treated with all the deference due to her past rank and did a roaring trade with the men who got a vicarious kick out of bedding with the old man's wife.

The brothel or BMC was an all-important institution and every unit possessed one, though the quantity and quality of the girls varied according to the district and the origin of the troops. The most sumptuous were those run by the North Africans, who seemed to have a positive genius in the matter.

The BMC for our Battalion was the main house with about twenty girls and supplied the companies according to their needs, on a rotation basis. In charge was the 'Madame' who controlled the general discipline of the girls and their clients. The house was widely patronised by all ranks including the officers, and she made an enormous turnover: the profits were controlled by the doctor who was charged with the medical inspection of the girls, the picking of them and the general layout of their quarters and health.

The girls were a merry, raddled, over-painted lot, though their duck-bottomed gait and generally tawdry appearance were rather nauseating. Cheerful and hardworking, they knew, biblically, very nearly everyone in the Battalion and gave not one damn for rank. The fact of being so intimately acquainted with the personnel of the Battalion developed in them a curiously acute *esprit de corps*: invariably invited to the officers and NCOs' messes for celebrations, they participated equally in those of the men promoted and decorated and wept bitterly over the dead or repatriated who had been good customers. Frequently the better-looking or more skilful left the BMC for a spell to become somebody's congaie: in which case the man bought up what was left of her contract from the Madame and the two set up house together.

Every now and again the Madame decided to prove her solidarity and to gainsay bitter tongues who accused her of being a skinflint and a robber. Christmas was one of them and the first that I had witnessed. It was a memorable and curiously lamentable

59

affair. On the afternoon of Christmas Eve we were all invited to a cocktail party in the BMC. A huge variety of drinks and sandwiches were handed round by the girls, who, all dressed up for the occasion, were treated with the utmost respect by everybody and were most mysterious about the second part of their programme. All that we could gather was that the Madame, with Baudoin's and Angeli's approval, had organised something that would take place just before midnight in conjunction with the Company's midnight Christmas revue.

As a special favour the Bande Noire and some Cambodian auxiliaries had been detailed to take over the guard and general duties for forty-eight hours, so, by the end of the Madame's cocktail party, we were able to continue the traditional overeating, drinking and general merrymaking to our hearts' content, while we waited for the variety show to begin in the canteen. Around eleven the curtain went up and the show began. During the intervals Baudoin handed out Christmas presents of wristwatches to his men—several of which caused instant interest and hilarity by running through twenty-four hours in about as many seconds. Christmas presents for the men was traditional in the Legion. The Company Commander bought them with the canteen profits. His own present was bought with money stopped from the men's pay. Just before midnight the bugler sounded off with a fantastic call of his own invention, the lights went out, the curtain up and there on the stage were the Madame and her girls prancing around in every variety of undress, carrying enormous cut-out paper letters, spelling out 'HAPPY CHRISTMAS TO YOU AND YOURS WHO ARE FAR AWAY'; the whole to a weird cacophony they were singing which vaguely resembled a mixture of 'Holy Night' and 'Auld Lang Syne'. The effect on the majority of us was appalling—somehow the sight of those raddled overpainted old bags touching on Christmas and home life was so unbelievably sinister and obscene that it killed the evening.

Baudoin never did understand why his Christmas show was a flop.

Chapter
5

BY CHRISTMAS I had been in Indochina for a little over two months and I was beginning to get acclimatised— a process which was as much psychological as physical, the heat, humidity and general way of life taking quite a bit of getting used to. The novelty of the surroundings and the fact that I was living at a very lively tempo had helped to offset the normally depressing first effects of the climate and the nervous tension engendered by finding myself in a completely hostile country— doubly so to a European in uniform.

From the day of my assignment to the CCB I had been swept into the life of the Company and, owing to the shortage of personnel, I managed to pack in a host of odd operational, escort and patrol outings. Later on pressure of work, idleness and indifference made me cut down a bit on all that, but, for the first three or four months I was there, any excuse was good enough to drop everything and go soldiering.

Early in November, at the tail end of the rainy season, and just after my first patrol with Thyme and the Son Cat episode, I was sent off with some stores for the rest of the Company which was out on a long-term operation. The Battalion was busy trying to get a post implanted about thirty miles away and the companies had stores sent up once a week from the bases.

I found myself in charge of a couple of trucks loaded down to the axles with food, beer, munitions and a live buffalo—the fresh meat supply. I had a couple of men as escort for each truck, the two drivers and myself. Once the stores were checked we took off. What I hadn't realised was that the thirty miles were crow's flight—not travelling distance. After a three-and-a-half-hour grind down tracks that were axle-deep in mud, through five consecutive cloudbursts and a couple of dozen 75-mm. shells, fired by a gunner trying to calculate his range and getting mixed up in direction, we arrived at the branch road where D Company held a post. Once there I was told that the Viet had cut the road and that I would have to take the trucks down to the river, which ran past the projected post later in its course, and off-load the stores into a boat which should be waiting for me. We arrived at the river to find that the boat wouldn't be there until the next morning. I got the trucks unloaded easily enough, except for the buffalo. Finally we took the hobbles off his legs and he hurtled to the ground.

The trouble then was to catch him. Next to a wild buffalo, the Indochinese domestic variety must be the meanest brute alive, and quick as a cat. After a longish chase and a short corrida, led by one of the men who was a Spaniard, we had him hobbled again. I kept one man to guard the stores—stacked in the shelter of a small post on the river bank—sent the trucks back to HQ and went off to find the gunner responsible for shooting us up. By the time he had finished making amends I was ready to fall into bed—it was no country for drinking.

In the morning an old scow turned up, escorted by a couple of river gunboats, and I got my stuff on board, including the buffalo who was just as cross-grained as ever. Unfortunately I was far from being alone—three other companies had also sent stores the same day. Without any livestock, thank God. We each sat on our pile hating each other the length of the two-hour trip, each convinced that the other's sole objective was to filch his beer. None of us were far wrong. We chugged up the river through rain storms and occasional Viet snipers' bullets, which drew an immediate riposte from the machine guns on the gunboats, until a primitive-looking landing stage hove in sight.

When we got hear enough, we saw that there was quite a crowd waiting for us and found out why all too soon. The men had been out of beer for over twenty-four hours and it was literally a boarding party that swept on to the poor old scow, offering to help unload the stores. After a lot of yelling and cursing I managed to get all my stuff together on to the trucks that had come down to meet me and I had to beat off the volunteers, who insisted on escorting me for the five-hundred-yard run from the river bank to the company bivouac. As it was, one driver, who knew I was a greenhorn, nearly sold a couple of cases which he had arranged to 'break' en route. I just stopped him in time.

I managed to get rid of the right things in the right places and to collect the different receipts and papers, without which the French Army would be immobilised, and finally unearthed Baudoin in a very soigné foxhole. I reported my presence and handed over the Company's mail. It was then well past midday so he said that I might as well spend the night there, since the road would be opened by next morning, and he could use me to take back a truck for repairs plus a couple of characters who were sick. The formalities being done with, I struggled back through the mud to the improvised canteen to have a couple of well-earned drinks and to find a bed for the night. The latter was not so easy.

The whole camp-site was a sea of mud, and dry spots were jealously guarded. In the end I persuaded Camus, who ran the canteen, to let me sleep on the beer cases. There were plenty of sacks which were only slightly damp and he had rigged up an enormous dugout under the tent which served as canteen and kitchen. It was at least as good as Baudoin's and twice as large.

The camp itself was in an abandoned rubber plantation and different companies were bivouaced in the shape of a crescent, with the horns running down to the river. In the middle was the emplacement for the future post, which was half finished. The outer edge of the bivouac was Viet country and they came in close at night to lob in mortar shells, or else lay mines along the tracks the patrols took in the mornings. On the whole, however, apart from the mud and the Viet, it was a pleasant place providing one didn't stay too long.

Camus was a sociable man, and he decided that since it was my first night to the camp, there ought to be a celebration. He made arrangements accordingly. Amongst other things that I had brought with the stores were a dozen large canisters full of live eels, destined for the partisans. Camus borrowed a few eels and put them in a smaller can, full of water—he explained that they were for a snack towards the end of the evening. Then he went to the kitchen and got a few simpler forms of eatables, hauled several bottles of wine and a couple of bottles of brandy from a private store and declared the proceedings open. Apart from Camus and I, there were two pals of his. The four of us set to with a will. We had to get down with the eating before dusk as the blackout was strict—we could drink in the dark all right, but eating became too complicated.

It was a good party, and by the time that we had gone through a few bottles of wine and polished off a bottle of brandy it was getting late. We decided to get some sleep and the others crept off to their holes while Camus and I dossed down in his place.

Either the brandy was very good or the sacks very soft, because I went straight off into a dreamless sleep. Not for long, however.

An unearthly demoniacal howl of anguish brought me off the cases on to my feet. I struck a match to get my bearings and looked over to where I could hear Camus struggling and gasping. From where I was it looked as though he were trying to strangle somebody and my first reaction was to grab a pistol. I was convinced that a Viet must have crept in past the sentries and was trying to kill Camus. I struck a second match and in a couple of strides was next to his bed. As I got there one of the characters who had been drinking with us came in with a flashlight—he too had been woken by the howl and had come over to see what had happened. At that moment Camus managed to splutter out a spate of curses and at the same time tell us what he was up to—by then we had realised that he was alone in bed. He had put the eels he had borrowed under his bed, and one of them had managed to slide up his trouser-leg while he was asleep—where it still was, but waist high. While Camus struggled and swore the two of us collapsed on to the beer cases, helpless with laughter. When we had 'come to' a bit, Camus had got the eel back into the can and had recovered his composure enough to call us a lot of names and offer us a drink. Five minutes later, after a cigarette and a reminiscent chuckle, I was sound asleep again.

The next reveille was equally abrupt. It must have been about four in the morning when I was woken up by a rapid succession of earth-rocking explosions and several sharp bursts of machine-gun fire. I started to get up but Camus said it wasn't worth while—just the nightly hymn of hate from the Viet to keep us aware of his presence. I was most relieved and sank back on to my sacks to sleep for the third time. A little after daybreak Baudoin's batman came down and told me that Baudoin wanted to see me before I left. I thought I might as well go straight away and left the canteen to wade across to Baudoin's dugout. As I left, Camus shouted that he would get breakfast ready and not to take too long.

I found Baudoin in bed, which didn't seem to worry him at all. He told me to be ready to leave at nine and added that I would have to take a walking wounded back as well as the two who were sick, then handed me out, from under his mosquito net, the papers that he was sending back and said goodbye. I left and went to hunt up the man who had been wounded.

He was in the infirmary tent lying flat on his belly and looking as pleased as Punch. He was a German peasant called Maier. He had only come up to the camp three days ago and hated every second of it. The Company had been short of men, and Maier, who had been left behind to look after the Company pigs, had suddenly found himself sent up to the camp. Pigs he could understand, but soldiering left him cold. On top of which he suffered from night blindness and couldn't stand sentry at night—which made the others in his platoon gripe. During the night he had been woken up by the mortar fire and had begun to fumble for his rifle when a whiplash across his buttocks had made him leap to his feet to catch the bastard who had hit him. It was then that he had felt a warm trickle of liquid running down his thighs. At first he thought that he had messed himself and dropped his pants to clean up, when he realised that it was blood. A splinter of mortar shell had creased his buttocks, just enough to keep him in hospital for a couple of months—on top of which he got a Croix de Guerre for gallantry and devotion to duty in spite of wounds sustained during a night attack. A few months later he stopped another splinter in the scalp, under almost identical circumstances, got a second Croix de Guerre and lived happily ever after as the most decorated pigman in Indochina.

By the time that I had waded back to the canteen I found Camus had uncorked a couple of bottles and was already eating. With a faint shudder I realised that the dish was stewed eels.

The trip back to HQ was uneventful. Even though nothing much had happened during the past forty-eight hours the strangeness of it all had hardly been a rest cure, and I was damn glad that I didn't have to do the trip a couple or three times a week.

I got rid of my papers, dumped the sick and wounded at the infirmary and went over to the office to suggest to Tranchant that I take the rest of the day off. Nothing doing—a neighbouring post had been through an all-night attack, lost, re-won, half-destroyed, saved, and God knows what else besides. Since I was already in combat gear I was to get a couple of men as escort, take a jeep and go over to the post to fetch the post commander's report on the night's doings.

It took us a fast twenty-minute jeep ride to reach the post of

Cat Bi where we found Adjutant Delbos, who had just come back for a third stay in Indochina. During his first two he had been promoted from Corporal to Adjutant and had amassed a chestful of decorations earned the hard way. As soon as he arrived he was given command of a commando and a post in a particularly tricky area of the sector.

The Viet had been driven out two years ago but had kept local contacts and were known to have had ideas about taking Cat Bi by surprise. Delbos accepted the fact as a fact and spent his first day getting acquainted with the post and with his NCOs, who were all Cambodian. The Viet attack came on his first night and within five minutes they had managed to get inside the fortifications and occupy the block-houses which formed the outer defences.

Delbos, reacting fast, got his men together in the main tower, and held the Viet off till dawn. Then he counter-attacked and in a wild hand-to-hand skirmish beat the Viet back out of the post and took ten prisoners. When the action was over he found that he had done all his fighting with a rifle used as club. He had reduced it to a twisted wreck. He was awarded another medal and at the same time an official reprimand for having been negligent enough to allow the Viet to penetrate his outer defences.

We took Delbos back with us to Battalion HQ to make his own verbal report, and Tranchant at last decided to let me call it a day.

Chapter
6

DECEMBER AND JANUARY were supposed to be the cool and pleasant months in Cochinchina, which was a matter of faith rather than fact. The temperature dropped 2 degrees. Boxing Day happened to be a day when the temperature seemed to have gone up and, to augment the feeling of his discomfort, Colonel Angeli broke the news to us that the Battalion was to change sector and that we had to get all plans prepared for the move and be installed in the new sector by New Year's Day. In spite of the champagne Angeli had offered us to offset the shock, and our collective hangover, we got the job done.

I was sent off a day in advance to prospect the new headquarters and to fix up a provisional office so that work could go on as usual without any delay. This was Tranchant's idea; he said he knew how much I liked travelling. Armed with a typewriter, carbons, paper, my gear and a thick head, I boarded one of the trucks that was already loaded with stores, and we set off. It was a forty-mile run down the main road towards Cambodia and from what I had gathered the extreme limits of the new sector where the Cambodian frontier and our former extreme boundary —as though our entire former sector had been turned over from right to left like the page of a book.

We got to Loc Ninh and found the post in complete confusion

—trucks, men and gear all over the place and everyone hot, dirty and bad-tempered. The outgoing troops were furious at the sudden move; so were we, but there was nothing we could do about it. Finally I located the HQ office, presented myself and asked where I could dump my gear and set up a provisional office for the Battalion. A harassed officer howled at me that I wasn't supposed to be there till the next day, so I snapped back that I had been sent in advance to make some sort of plan for the move in. After a few minutes of bickering he realised that I was very small fry and, cooling off a bit, allocated me an office— four bare walls that were crumbling, a broken window and a drunken-looking door.

The outgoing unit was a North African cavalry regiment, and the Arabs were leaving nothing behind except mountains of evil-smelling fly-blown detritus, choked drains and vermin. Feeling hot, disgusted and liverish, I scrawled a brief report to Tranchant, warning him what to expect. Then I barricaded the door of the 'office' as best I could, so that the Arabs couldn't move out my stuff as well as theirs, and went off to find a Battalion- bound driver. That done, I wandered around in the hopes of finding a shower, but even the showers had been dismantled. Tired, hotter than ever, thirsty and in open revolt I left the post and went out into the village—it was midday and the sun was just getting into full egg-frying swing.

I found a general store which looked bigger and cleaner than the other village buildings and went in to find out where one could eat, drink, wash and relax in peace for an hour or two. Blinded from the white heat outside, I saw nothing at first, then from the cool darkness of the store I saw coming towards me a bobbing, bowing, chubby bespectacled little man. In a flowery French he asked me to make his house my own and what could he do for me. A bit shaken by this sudden and unexpected amiability, I explained that I was dying for a shower, a cool drink and somewhere to sit out the siesta. Towels, soap, and a sarong were in my hands before I had finished speaking and I was being ushered through the store and the back of the house and out into the courtyard. He apologised profusely for the humbleness of his showering installations, then left me in a little brick bath-house. There was a cement-lined tank full of deliciously cool, clean water and a coconut-shell-dipper for scooping and pouring.

Ten minutes later, refreshed and feeling almost human, I was sitting in his parlour-bar-restaurant sipping beer and nibbling dried shrimps, octopus and pickled garlic while we fenced around trying to find out what mutual use we could be to each other.

Nguyen van Thieu was a pleasant little man, but resourceful, astute and nobody's fool. He had seen the village change hands so often that he had learned to trim his sails accordingly. Foreign Legion, Caodai, North Africans, French colonials came and saw while Thieu stayed and conquered—a chubby welcoming smile lighting his face whilst behind his enormous horn-rimmed spectacles his eyes calculated with lightning rapidity the financial possibilities of every new arrival.

He had changed trades so often that it was hard to know what he didn't do. Once he started a new line he never let it drop, altogether.

He was a State-qualified teacher and ran a school for the children of the wealthier local tradesmen and notabilities, but employed another teacher to do the work. He had owned and run a small passenger and trucking service until rival concerns had smashed up his vehicles, but, even without, he still dabbled in the trucking trade. He had converted the front of his house into a general store and in the parlour had installed a bar-restaurant 'for the use of the better-class people', as he put it. In his back yard he had built an enormous baker's oven and had managed to pull in army bread contracts from neighbouring posts and villages; coupled with which he ran a lucrative sideline in fish, poultry, eggs and vegetables. He had shares in the only ice-cream factory in the district and it was run by his nephew. His brother was a local master carpenter and between them they had cornered the market in the coffin trade. His step-brother had inherited the local salt monopoly and they had organised a fish-salting and nuoc mam factory of some size (nuoc mam was an amber-coloured liquid obtained by pressing alternate layers of coarse salt and rotting fish; the evil-smelling juice which ran off was a principal and indispensable part of the Annamite diet—rice—nuoc mam—dried fish—and tasted far better than it smelled).

All in all, Nguyen van Thieu was a very useful man to know. But the poor chap lived in a state of constant torment owing to the multiplicity of his interests. The highly volatile state of current prices meant that he had to spend hours a day adding and sub-tracting, multiplying and dividing in order to break even. Salt went down a point and he was ruined, flour up a penny and he was saved, etc. . . . Through the ceaseless whirlpool of his hurried calculations and frenzied additions floated his wife.

Of an old aristocratic family, she considered the dealings of her husband with an amused and disdainful eye—these tradesmen . . . ugh! Calm and lovely, she rarely raised her voice above a fluting whisper, never hurried and was always dressed in the traditional trousers and long, neck-high coats which fitted like a glove. The only outward sign of interest she took in his affairs was counting the receipts at the end of the day. With delicate fingers and a slender, disgusted half-smile, she counted and locked away the day's taking in an enormous Victorian cast-iron safe; once the cash was in there Thieu had the devil's own job to get any of it back.

His main trouble was his overwhelming desire to get rich quick, though he did have the sense to stifle the innate passion of every Annamite for gambling. Ambitious, he had sent his eldest son to a university in France and his three daughters to a Catholic convent in Saigon. Astute, he admitted publicly to no definite political attachment. In fact he represented the bulk of the Annamite mercantile class and his store and multifarious business activities were the reflection of his political beliefs—a little of something for every taste. His drinks ranged from 'genuine'

Scotch brewed and bottled in Cholon to local jungle-juice; his restaurant from canned lobster to peanuts: his store from imitation silk kimonos to army socks—from phoney Parker 51s to Chinese brush-pens and from penicillin to local herb medicines. There was everything there and most of it bad, but it sold.

Some of all that I picked up during my first meeting with Thieu, but most later. I was to see a lot of him and we became fairly good friends.

By the time we had finished the beer and weighing each other up it was time for me to get back to work. Before I left he invited me to dinner and to stay the night if I had no bed. I accepted the dinner.

The rest of the day I spent racketing around trying to get the hang of the new post. It covered an enormous area, in comparison to our old one, and seemed wildly impractical at first sight. Right in the middle and cutting it into two halves was the local high school, neatly fenced off by barbed wire; in another corner I found the local police station and the Police Commissioner's bungalow. There were buildings all over the place, each more run-down and dilapidated that the other. The North Africans seemed determined to leave nothing habitable. I finally managed to dig out a building or two that looked as though they were waterproof and capable of holding the different stores and furniture for the night, and rounded up some prisoners to move it all in. That done, I decided to knock off for the day—I was my own boss till the next morning.

Worn out by Christmas, the heat and the general fatigue of moving into a strange place, I dragged myself wearily back to Thieu's in the hope of a good meal and a few quiet drinks before the curfew. When I got there he came out bowing and bobbing, wreathed in smiles and treating me like an old and well-established family friend—it was very pleasant. However, as we went into the store, he pulled me into a corner and hissed feverishly into my ear that there was a friend of his there he wanted me to meet, 'one of the better-class people', a frequenter of the bar-restaurant,

a very nice man, the Police Commissioner himself—and added
that as it was a special occasion the Commissioner and I were
to be his guests. My finances being pretty low, it sounded a wonderful idea and, Police Commissioner or no, I accepted readily.
Thieu, finished with his palaver, led me on through into the
resort of the better-class people and introduced me to Commissioner Blanchet, who was just finishing a drink, then bustled
about setting out more drinks and disappeared discreetly while
we got to know each other.

Blanchet was a smallish man, compact and curly-haired,
with a slow wide grin and intelligent humorous eyes. We
observed a formula current in Indochina—a form of Expeditionary Force check-up, which enabled us to place each other in our
respective spheres of activity, and after a little general conversation I asked him to give me the low-down on the sector which
for me was an unknown quantity. He warned me that it was a
fairly complicated question, and then launched into a general
survey.

The whole area from Loc Ninh to the Cambodian frontier,
some fifty miles away, was the acknowledged fief of the Caodaists. The Caodaists, though Annamite, formed an independent
religious and politico-military sect and were immensely rich
and powerful. They played a complex role—officially allies of
the French Union forces, they were at the same time on not
unfriendly terms with the Vietminh and on definitely inimical
terms with the official Baodai government, whom they reproached for being too friendly towards the French. They ran a
small well-armed army, most of the armament coming from the
French, and held posts and towers throughout the sector. Certain
areas they guarded jealously for themselves and were bitterly
hostile to any idea that French troops should circulate within
them. They refused to pay national taxes and, conversely, levied
illegal local taxes off the peasants, tradesmen and transport
concerns within their areas of influence.

The headquarters of the Caodaist movement were at Tay

Ninh, about forty miles away, but in the village of Loc Ninh itself they kept a garrison of near battalion strength which served as the local Caodai rallying point and cut the village into two unofficial sections. It was unwise for Europeans or French auxiliary troops to circulate in the Caodai section of the village. Blanchet himself was in a very delicate situation. His predecessor had been assassinated the previous September and the assassin was known to have been a Caodai or a man in their pay. He had been killed because he had tried to arrest a man wanted for questioning and whom he knew to be sheltering in the Caodai sector. He had gone to get his man but never came back alive.

Blanchet realised that, even though his position gave him the official right to conduct an investigation in the Caodai sector, it would be extremely unwise to follow the same course as his predecessor. He had managed, after a lot of diplomatic small talk, to establish an uneasy *status quo* with the Caodai by which they agreed to keep out of each other's hair and to turn over undesirables when the case came up. However, he never went into their sector without a heavily-armed escort and insisted that they came to his office when there was any official business to discuss. As representative of French justice for a large area his official rating was high enough for them to comply with this without loss of face.

It appeared that the North Africans whom we were relieving had allowed the Caodaists to do much as they pleased and he was both amused and interested to see what would happen once the Legion had taken the sector in hand. He knew from past experience that it was unlikely that we would allow them a free hand and seemed convinced that there would be trouble in the near future.

By the time Blanchet had got that far, Thieu had locked up his shop and he and his wife were bringing in a battery of steaming bowls and dishes. The table laid, we fell to with chopsticks, and soon polished off an excellent and succulent meal—just in time to get back to the post before the curfew.

The next day, New Year's Eve, the rest of the headquarters staff and the CCB arrived with the stores, gear and furniture. The day was taken up installing offices and rooms and getting through with the most urgent work before the New Year celebrations fell on us. It promised to be a hectic New Year, as Major Angeli was being promoted to Colonel, which meant an added celebration to the one that we had already planned for Tranchant, who was promoted to Warrant Officer.

About seven in the evening, however, there was a call for volunteers to go out on an ambush. The Bande Noire had gathered the information that an important Viet supply convoy, which had left Saigon two days previously, was expected to pass the outskirts of a Caodai village six miles away around midnight. The convoy was obviously taking advantage of the fact that the sector had just changed hands, and would stick closely to a well-established route. However, it was not felt to be wise to entrust the ambush to the Bande Noire. Colonel Angeli was none too sure what the Caodai reaction to them might be and incidents were to be avoided for the time being.

We left the post at nine o'clock, and set off down the road in the direction of Suoi Da, the village in question. It was Sergeant Thyme's platoon, and since he was again short of a group leader, I went along. After a two-hour march we reached the outskirts of Suoi Da, which was held by the Caodaists. Thyme, the interpreter and one group went up to the outer defences to identify the patrol and get the *chevaux de frise* opened while the rest of us dropped into the ditches on either side of the road. The Caodai headquarters at Loc Ninh had been telephoned and told to warn the village of our arrival and, before leaving, Thyme had rechecked on that to make sure that we wouldn't run into a welcoming committee opening up on us with machine-guns. Even so, none of us felt very confident about the Caodai.

Since our departure from the post, all had been carried out in the utmost silence, so as not to betray our presence, but as soon as Thyme and the others got near to the *chevaux de frise* to give the password and patrol identity, the silence was shattered by a ribald yell from the Caodai side of the defences. Thyme was told, in pidgin French, to get the hell out of there and fast—otherwise we would be fired on. The threat was followed by the all-too-audible click and clack of automatic arms being brought to the ready. Dancing with rage, Thyme controlled himself as best he could and tried once again to give the password and patrol identity as quietly as possible. At the same time he told the interpreter to ask for a responsible officer to come and parley, to say that our passage had been arranged by 'phone and that it had been okayed by the Caodaist Headquarters. A cold little voice answered, very icily, that Thyme had just thirty seconds in which to about-face his men and get the hell out of there; if not, the automatic weapons in the watch-tower would open up. Trembling with suppressed rage and humiliation, Thyme tried yet again to make himself heard—the only answer was the click of a rifle-bolt being shot home.

Once out of the line of fire, we gathered and discussed the possibility of skirting the village but, since none of us knew the local topography well enough, Thyme judged that it was inadvisable. The Caodai were quite obviously itching to have a crack at us and he didn't dare risk a mêlée with them on his first sortie into their territory—he had received orders to avoid all action which would engender friction. Furious and disappointed—the convoy was an important one—we turned and headed for home. As we started off there was a crash and a lot of muffled cursing. One of the men had caught his foot in a piece of stray wire and had fallen; while we were disentangling him we realised that it was the end of a telephone line freshly cut. We followed it up to within a stone's throw of the outer defences of Suoi Da. The discovery made sudden sense of the refusal to let us through the village and backed up what we heard about Caodai double-dealing. There was no doubt that they had received a warning that we were passing through to lay an ambush the other side of the village and had, with the unofficial approval

of their HQ, cut the line afterwards. That way they could dis-
claim any knowledge of our accorded passage, tip off the Viets
that they had countered our ambush plans and collect a rake-off
for services rendered. As we trudged off back to the post, tom-
toms began to beat derisively behind us.

It was our first run-in with our new allies and it was to set the
tone for our future relations with them.

Chapter
7

THE COFFEE-SHOPS and market stalls in the village opened at the crack of dawn and, when I went out for breakfast about six-thirty, the whole place seemed to know about our setback the night before. An air of uncanny expectancy hung over the crowds of peasants and vendors, who were obviously waiting to see what the official reaction would be.

The answer was not long in coming.

I had barely got back to the office when Colonel Angeli called for me. Tranchant had been given the day off to celebrate his promotion to Warrant Officer and I was replacing him. The Colonel told me to go and find the liaison officer and ask him to come down to the office immediately. Attached to the Battalion was a French officer responsible for liaison and general relations with the Caodai. As soon as he arrived, the Colonel asked him to ring up the Caodai headquarters and to warn the Caodai Colonel—or Trung Ta—that the Colonel commanding the sector expected to see him at sector headquarters within the briefest delay. I made myself as small as possible and stayed to watch the fun.

The Trung Ta arrived by jeep five minutes later and was told quite bluntly that, if any other incident occurred—of the same nature as that which had occurred the previous night—the post or tower or unit of the Caodai troops in question would be considered hostile; that the troops under his command had been instructed to take any action necessary for the successful accomplishment of their future missions.

It was blunt talk and to the point, and went down very badly. The liaison officer hopped about trying to soften the tone, so that the Trung Ta would not feel he was losing face, but Angeli, newly promoted to Colonel, was adamant. The Trung Ta left with a good-sized flea in the ear and another spoke went into the wheel of Franco-Caodai good relations.

I saw Blanchet later in the day and he grinned from ear to ear when he asked, in an offhand way, if I understood a little more about the Caodai problem.

Incidents multiplied and the tension grew throughout January. Several of the Battalion congaies, who were coming to Loc Ninh in a lorry they had hired, were stopped at the entrance to the village by a Caodai patrol and forced to get off the lorry with their baggage. The lorry was sent on. The women were then told that they were suspected of being Viet agents and were stripped and searched for documents, arms, etc. During the search, which was bawdy and none too delicate, most of their valuables disappeared. Finally they were released and allowed to continue their way on foot. The reaction amongst their men-folk in the Battalion was violent, and serious trouble was narrowly avoided. Evidently the Caodai were officially in the right and the Legion frequently did the same. The former knew however that the women belonged to the Battalion and their bawdy brutality, according to local standards, caused an automatic loss of face for the husbands.

Frequently when our night patrols left the village through the Caodai section, the latter made such a racket opening and shutting the *chevaux de frise* and road-blocks that the secrecy of the patrol was dissolved before the patrol had got clear of the village and, to complete the good work, they would play searchlights on us as we went off into the country. If we complained they would

79

blandly reply that they had heard odd noises and suspected the approach of hostile elements.

Then in February the Trung Ta made an official request that two men of the Bande Noire should be handed over to his HQ for questioning. They were, he said, suspected of having taken part in the murder of a Caodai officer and were known criminals and Viet agents. All of which was perfectly well known at Battalion HQ. They were invaluable to us—renegade Viets, they were two of the best agents the Battalion possessed. As a result of the request they had to be hidden discreetly, till the Trung Ta thought up something else. We sent a reply that the men must have suspected something as they had deserted but that they would be handed over if recaptured alive. The next round, however, went to the Legion.

A neighbouring post held by a commando sent out a patrol early one morning. After a while the patrol spotted a bullock-cart convoy. The patrol got into position and opened fire on the carts—the carts scattered in all directions and the escorting troops returned heavy fire. After a short sharp skirmish lasting a few minutes the Viet broke off the action and, melting into the surrounding country, disappeared. On the terrain, from which the Viet had been firing, the patrol found several dead and badly wounded—not Viet but Caodai who had been escorting the Viet convoy through French territory. At Battalion HQ we never heard the slightest word about the matter from the Trung Ta.

Surely and rapidly the tension grew, and by the end of February every day brought some new pinprick or cudgel blow from one side or the other. One morning a French-paid auxiliary was coming off sentry duty at a crossroad near the centre of the village, leading a buffalo he had put out to graze round his post during his turn of duty. It was early and he was half-asleep, ambling along with the buffalo's halter in one hand and his tommy-gun over the other shoulder. Suddenly someone sprang on him from behind, knocked him into the ditch at the side of the road, snatched up his tommy-gun and raced off up the road towards the Caodai garrison. The buffalo just disappeared. A local policeman, stationed at the crossroads, saw the last part of the aggression and opened fire on the fugitive with his revolver. A Caodai sentinel, stationed further up the road, immediately opened fire with his Sten but fired at the policeman and the auxiliary, who were obliged to leap into the ditch and crawl along it until they were out of the line of fire, before being able to get up and run to Battalion HQ to report the incident.

There was the hell of a row. Blanchet, the Police Commissioner, came round to see Colonel Angeli and asked that action be taken at once as one of his men had been fired at. They rang up the Trung Ta and insisted that he should turn over the aggressor and the stolen weapon immediately and that the Caodai sentry who had fired on the two men should be severely punished. The Trung Ta calmly promised to ascertain whether or not one of his men had been guilty of the aggression, though he for his part had heard nothing about it in his section of the village. He refused, however, to hear of punishing the sentinel who, he said, had seen nobody running towards him. He had imagined that he was being attacked when he heard bullets whistling over his head, and had acted purely in self-defence.

Later that day a Caodaist Lieutenant drove up to Battalion HQ with a tommy-gun and asked if it was the one which had disappeared that morning. It had, he said, been recuperated from the body of a Viet saboteur shot down during the afternoon by a Caodai patrol. The arm proved to be the one in question and the incident was officially closed, though not forgotten, with face-saving all round. The Bande Noire brought in the information, later verified, two days afterwards that the Viet saboteur, shot down by the Caodai, was none other than an auxiliary the Caodai had kidnapped some weeks earlier. He had been officially reported missing or deserted but had been taken by the Caodai in settlement of some private feud. In order not to lose face, by bringing in the missing weapon too easily, they had shot the auxiliary and then dumped the body in a paddy-field with the weapon and sent out a patrol to find it.

These and a lot of other incidents were an infernal nuisance and made life in the post and the village most unpleasant. They had been going on about six weeks when I was sent down to Saigon to deliver an urgent report to GHQ. As our transport situation was bad I went down with the truck which handled beer and stores for the CCB. Once the note was delivered I had a few hours in which to roam around. It was wonderful to escape from the tension of Loc Ninh even for so short a while. I found the truck ready to leave Saigon about three o'clock, climbed up on to the beer crates and settled down in a state of torpor due as much to having overeaten as to the heat.

Lying on top of the beer crates with me was Newmann. As the truck snorted and groaned its heavily laden old carcase back to the post, Newmann and I basked in the sun, and he philosophised lazily while we balanced to the jolts and swaying of the truck.

Beer, he maintained, was as vital as bullets when men were out all day sweating and struggling through brush and paddy-fields. Beer cut through the accumulated fatigue and thirst piled up by the sun—beer let taut nerves unwind and jangle pleasantly —even when not ice-cold, just cool, it tasted better than water. Beer in fact was a number one must for the life and morale of any fighting unit. But beer didn't just walk around by itself waiting to be opened and sluiced down—it had to be fetched, carried, cooled by someone, and that someone was Lance-Sergeant Newmann, ten years' service and two years in Indochina on the beer-run. All of which made Newmann feel pretty good and very VIP, even though we were tooling along the main Saigon-Cambodia highway perched on top of a pile of beer-crates in an antiquated GMC.

The way he figured things out anyone could be a hero; it was just a matter of simple arithmetic. If a man went out Viet hunting six or seven days a week, every week in the year, by all laws of average one of two things was bound to happen. Either he got the Viet or the Viet got him, and in either case it meant a Croix de Guerre, which meant the birth or maybe the death of another hero. But no one could go out six or seven days weekly indefinitely, unless there was beer to come back to—nerves went wrong, men got trigger-happy, concentration became impossible. All of which made Newmann feel even better. He brought the beer back from Saigon seven days a week and so contributed to the success of the fighting man. All in all, he felt that he was as much of a hero as any of the others. I let him ramble on, feeling far too sleepy to do anything but grunt from time to time.

Newmann had just reached the stage in his reflections where he felt at peace with the world and himself when there came the roaring screeching blast of an explosion and torn metal. The truck came to an abrupt and violent halt, amidst the confused noises of breaking glass, vitriolic oaths from the driver and the stink of cordite and burning rubber. Newmann and I had been catapulted off the cases by the shock and we landed in the mud and water of the paddy-field. We groped around for our rifles, which had been jolted out of the crooks of our arms. Then, realising that there was no firing, we scrambled up on to the road.

The driver had already waved a following truck to a stop. There was a village held by a commando about five hundred yards down the road, so he boarded the truck and went off to get some help. Newmann and I stayed behind with the wreckage. Before poking around to see if anything was left intact, we tried to rub off a bit of the mud from the paddy-field; we were covered with it from head to foot. I had just finished with my face and was about to start on the rest when I took a look at Newmann, who was gazing in astonishment at his hands; they were covered with blood. I looked a bit closer and saw that he had a great gash on his forehead—a sliver of glass from one of the broken bottles must have got him before we were thrown off. I sat him down and patched him as best I could But Newmann, poor Newmann, was struck by only one fact. The beer, *his beer*, had been blown up by a mine. He got a decoration, though, and wore it.

Our driver soon came back with a group from the commando and a truck which the NCO in charge had commandeered from a Chinaman in the village. As the men loaded up what was left of our cargo the NCO told us that that particular section of the road should have been de-mined by the Caodai, who also had a small post in the village. The information didn't make us feel any more tender towards our 'allies', and I was furious. I didn't even have an honourable scar to show. All I got from the deal was a free mud-bath.

Chapter
8

THE FIRST BIG set-to with the Caodai came on a Sunday morning early in March and was to prove itself the precursor of far more serious trouble. As on most Sundays, the shops and stores were flag-bedecked and the streets were crowded with shoppers, pedlars, peasants and bunches of Légionnaires, Caodai, and Annamite auxiliaries in their best Sunday get-ups spending the day in town.

At the Battalion HQ all was quiet.

I was going to be promoted to Lance-Sergeant at the end of the month and Tranchant, who was due for repatriation, had handed me over his job of Battalion Sergeant-Major. I was in the office running through the different files to get the hang of things and was working away when suddenly two NCOs came in and asked for Lieutenant Blairot. Blairot was in Saigon with his wife, so I asked them to wait and sent an orderly to fetch Sergeant Estaing. They turned out to be security agents from Saigon who were checking on the activities of a Caodai Adjutant, suspected of dissidence and relations with the Viet. They knew that he would be in the village that day and they wanted to bring him in for questioning, but needed help. Estaing went off to get Colonel Angeli's consent and as soon as he came back with it they made a plan of action. Then Estaing sent for the available members of the Bande Noire and briefed them with a description of the wanted man, warning them to bring him in alive, though he didn't stress the question of the use of arms. The Saigon security men insisted on the need for caution and the necessity for absolute discretion.

The Bande Noire, when on duty in the village, always wore the traditional black cotton trousers and jackets, with a revolver or two tucked into the waistband and covered by the jacket— too many had scores to settle with them for it to be healthy for them to go out unarmed, even though it was forbidden to carry arms in the village without Blanchet's permission. They were, moreover, far too eager to have a crack at the Caodai to worry overmuch about Blanchet's authorisation.

A dozen of them left the post with Estaing to find the man. Estaing sat down at a café terrace in the centre of the village while the others paired off and began the hunt. The remaining dozen, feeling trouble in the air, sloped off to their quarters to pick up their tommy-guns and cartridge belts and came back to hang around the HQ office on the off-chance that their colleagues would run into difficulties in town.

Estaing and his men had only been gone a few minutes when I heard the sound of shooting coming from the direction of the market place, followed by a confused screaming and shouting as a stream of panic-stricken natives and unarmed soldiers came dashing down the road towards the post. The Bande Noire men with tommy-guns leapt out into the road and started to fire on every Caodai soldier within sight, at the same time spraying the shop fronts with stray bursts. Within a few seconds the sentries on duty had alerted the others and men were streaming out of their quarters at the double, and armed. A rapidly-formed patrol took off in the direction of the market to stop the shooting and quell the panic. When we got to the market, about a hundred yards from the post, the fighting was over and the place deserted except for three Caodai corpses in uniform, holding lonely court in the middle of the empty road, and a couple of peasant women, who had been wounded, groaning and whimpering on the pavement.

Picking up the dead and wounded, we loaded them on to a couple of abandoned handcarts and took them back to the post. By that time the firing had stopped, but the company was under arms. Machine-guns had been placed in battery facing the Caodai section of the village and groups of men were in position at strategic points of the village. The other side of the bridge, in the Caodai section, the Caodai had taken the same precautions and the village was to all intents and purposes ready for combat; even the main Saigon-Cambodia high road which ran through the village was sealed off and traffic was piling up at both ends.

Colonel Angeli and the Trung Ta had contacted each other by phone and had agreed to avoid further trouble at all costs. Both sides called in their armed troops and the village began to breathe again and life to continue a normal, if somewhat watchful, course. The first check-up on the affair gave Caodai losses at five killed, eight wounded, two of them seriously, four civilians wounded and, for the Battalion, one member of the Bande Noire with a bullet through the calf of his leg. (A later unofficial estimate gave at least twenty Caodai wounded, ten seriously, a figure concealed by the Caodai in order to save face.)

Within half an hour we had a fairly complete story of the events which could, unfortunately, be coloured to suit the tastes of the teller according to his point of view. The rest of the morning I spent writing and rewriting reports on the incident. The news had already reached Saigon and GHQ was screaming for a guilty head on which to hang the responsibility. The story broke down as follows.

Estaing sat down at the terrace of a café in the centre of the village—it was a good central spot, it was Sunday and he could sit there and watch without being noticed. He sent his men off in pairs, and the six couples began to saunter slowly through the crowds towards the market—being dressed in the traditional native clothes, they attracted little attention.

Suddenly one of them recognised the man they were looking for and, by signs, called over three of the other couples and discreetly pointed him out to them. He was in the uniform of a Caodai adjutant and was standing at a lemonade booth with a couple of other Caodai NCOs. They separated and closed in on the group. The man who had recognised the Adjutant first tapped him lightly on the shoulder; he turned and apparently, as soon as he saw the men around him, made a rapid move towards his pocket as though he was going to pull a gun. The men of the Bande Noire riddled him with bullets before he could pull the gun, and at the same time shot down one of the two NCOs who had also tried to pull a gun—the third managed to escape in the crowd. According to the Bande Noire, all three had been armed and had tried to pull their arms first. The sudden shooting panicked the crowd and as they scattered in all directions the Bande Noire shot at several other Caodai in 'self-defence'.

By the time Estaing had reached the scene the damage had already been done, and calling his men to heel, he took them back to the post to avoid further incidents. Those of the Bande Noire who had waited behind at the post thinking that their comrades had been attacked had raced out to the rescue and had only stopped firing when Colonel Angeli, alerted by the racket, had in his turn come running out and ordered them back into the post. The whole action, which had not taken over five minutes, had been caused by the Caodai Adjutant making for his gun, which was in itself illegal off-duty and in uniform within the village boundaries. That was the first official version.

Blanchet as Police Commissioner, however, was also vitally interested in the affair and had been in town when it had started. Armed men out of uniform shooting down allied troops and wounding civilians was quite definitely a matter for the police as well as for the military authorities, and he had his knife in the Bande Noire for several different shady deals they had pulled off. He was on the job as fast as the first military patrol, which had been sent down to the market to quell the trouble. From his first rapid survey and questioning of householders and other witnesses, it came out that not only were the three Caodai killed in the market place unarmed—there was no trace of arms, holsters, cartridge clips either on the bodies or in their immediate vicinity, nor had they been seen to pull a gun—but also that none of the other Caodai in flight had been seen to fire a shot or pull a gun.

The shooting had been done entirely by men dressed in civilian clothes and believed to belong to the section of special security agents attached to the Battalion. Moreover the only weapon which could be considered offensive found on the body of the Adjutant, had been a child's one-bladed penknife. Which made a bit of a hash of the first official version despatched to GHQ Saigon, as Blanchet's report would have the same destination.

Meanwhile the Trung Ta, heavily escorted, had made his appearance at Battalion HQ. He stalked into the office surrounded by an armed bodyguard of four tough-looking characters, slapped down his version of the affair and demanded the immediate punishment of those responsible for the shooting down of his men and retribution for the families of those killed. Nothing very definite came of the interview, and after a lot of stalling and double-talk he slammed out in a raging temper and hell-bent on revenge.

The whole affair had incurred the most appalling loss of face for the Caodai and local custom expected an eye for an eye. Colonel Angeli was in the devil of a pickle. It was impossible to explain to the Trung Ta that the origin of the affair was the attempted arrest of one of his men suspected of intelligence with the Viet and dissidence. Logically the Trung Ta should have been warned, and not having done so implied lack of confidence in his loyalty. It could not be put down to a simple outburst on the part of the Bande Noire or he would be obliged to disband his information service and anyway Saigon had asked for the maximum of discretion to avoid pushing the Caodai to dissidence.

To crown it all, Blanchet's report clearly implicated the Bande Noire as the cause of all the trouble and as Police Commissioner he could push the matter till it came up before the High Court—unless he were officially let into the real reason for the shooting of the Adjutant. Finally a report was cooked up pointing out that this last incident, unfortunately serious, was but one of a series which had been occurring since the battalion took over the sector. That the Police Commissioner's theory that the Caodai NCO had been unarmed was offset by the evidence of the Battalion security agents and that the weapons of the three dead Caodai in the market place had undoubtedly been hastily removed by Caodai sympathisers. That a large part of the blame could be attributed to the Caodai, who did everything within their power to aggravate the general tension and added that the Trung Ta was aware of the duplicity of the defunct Adjutant in question and was himself on the verge of dissidence.

Eventually the affair was lost sight of beneath a mountain of reports and was unofficially classified as settled, no sanctions were taken and life went on as normal.

Later in the week, however, the Caodai retaliated by placing a time-bomb in the market, wounding seventy-odd civilians. It was officially accepted that the bomb had been placed by a Viet terrorist and the matter was shelved. Security measures within the Battalion were tightened and all units warned to expect trouble and to reduce contact with the Caodai to the strict necessary minimum.

On our arrival in the new sector we had been faced with complications enough, thanks to our Caodai allies and their attitude towards the French, and to add a zest to the cocktail of conflicting interests there was yet another factor—that of the dissenting Caodai army.

A Caodai General named Tre had, some time previously, had a row with the Caodaic Pope who was the temporal as well as spiritual leader of the sect. He reproached the Pope for maintaining relations with the French on too friendly a basis and for being too co-operative with the Bao Dai régime. He insisted that the Caodai should become a free and independent state owing allegiance to none.

Popular in Caodai army circles, his attitude towards the Pope was backed by a considerable following of officers and men and, when the Pope refused to concede to his requests, he broke off relations with the Tay Ninh government and led his followers into the jungle. With them they took large stocks of arms, ammunitions and supplies as well as their wives and families and set up a dissenting sect which, though keeping the Caodai religion, broke completely with the politico-military concepts of the Tay Ninh or pure Caodaists.

Complicated enough as a situation to deal with, the matter was further confused by the fact that the dissenting troops had stayed on friendly relations with the regular Caodai troops. The dissenters frequently replenished their stock of supplies and ammunitions at the more obscure Caodai posts and even used these posts as rest-camps for those of the dissenters who were sick or wounded.

Tre kept his army out in the brush without any fixed base and warred impartially on the French, the Viet, and even the regular Caodai if the latter refused to supply him with his needs or proved in the least unco-operative. With the Viet he seemed to have come to a vague working agreement to concert joint action against the French, but the alliance was uneasy and prone to breaks. The one certainty that could be counted on was his unswerving hostility to the French and the Bao Dai régime.

The sector which the Battalion had taken over was largely implanted with Caodai posts and towers and the villages and roads they controlled were strictly their affair. We rarely went into their territory unless it was for some large-scale operation and had no means of controlling the presence or activity of the dissenting army unless called in by the Trung Ta; our Colonel knew, however, from local sources of information and from high-level warnings that the situation was delicate and that any moment there might be a sudden large-scale swing towards dissidence with the Trung Ta in the lead.

In fact it was that which happened a few days after the Sunday massacre. Relations between the two sections of the village had deteriorated to the point where the Caodai never came into the French section and even went fully armed in their own. No European could circulate in safety in the Caodai sector and the only contact between the two camps was that of Colonel Angeli and the Trung Ta by telephone. The villagers themselves reflected the growing tension—the slightest backfire of jeep or truck and the shutters went up, doors banged to and the streets emptied in a flash. The locals were too wise in the ways of war to take any risks. Reports from neighbouring posts and village indicated that the rise in tension was general and that the uneasiness was spreading throughout the sector—but the only thing to do was to sit and wait. The slightest move to disarm the Caodai or to relieve the post they held and a full-blooded war would have broken out through the length and breadth of Caodai territory with the French as objective number one.

Up till then Tre's dissenting army had employed the same tactics as the Viet and the danger he represented had never got out of hand. Fluid guerilla activity against isolated posts and small units and an absolute refusal to engage in a large-scale action was the system, and his army remained elusive and unfindable, in spite of several important sweeping movements at brigade and division level. Pinning down Tre was a task rendered doubly difficult owing to the fact that he was kept informed of all troop movements, of which he could be the objective, by sympathisers on the Caodai general staff.

In the last week of March the long-expected break came suddenly and dramatically at dawn one morning. The first news was brought by a haggard, bloodstained Caodai officer who came staggering into the Battalion HQ and announced that his men had mutinied and had made off with all the armament and ammunition of his post. They had set fire to the post and, before they left, they had given him a severe beating because he would not join them. I warned Colonel Angeli and the liaison officer immediately and they both telephoned to the Trung Ta to demand an explanation as to why *he* had not warned them. The Trung Ta sounded most surprised, excused himself and rang off—a few minutes later he called up the Battalion and reported that the majority of the men in the garrison had disappeared and that only three of his fourteen officers were present. He added that a large quantity of armament and ammunition had disappeared as well.

For the rest of the day news kept on coming in that throughout the sector the same thing had happened. In some posts the Caodai had left *en bloc*, in other there had been fighting, in others beatings and in yet others men had just slipped away in the night. From the various reports it became obvious that the dissidents were heading for the forest of Boi Loi, a wild and savage region where Tre was suspected of having his HQ.

A scratch combat battalion was hastily put on foot and we set off in pursuit of the deserters early the following day. After three days of fruitless searching we returned, having managed to surprise only one small group and even that gave us the slip, leaving a few dead behind.

Chapter
9

Meanwhile the Tay Ninh headquarters of the Caodai had been contacted and fresh Caodai troops were sent down to the sector to take over the posts and towers. A clean sweep was made, the Trung Ta, his officers and the few men who had not deserted being sent back to Tay Ninh. For all that the situation remained very confused and uncertain for a while and the utmost suspicion reigned in all that concerned the Caodai. Colonel Angeli, as sector commander, issued a temporary standing order that Caodaist activities were to be limited to the guarding of their posts and towers and that all troop movement or patrols were strictly forbidden to the Caodai unless he gave his express permission. He warned the Trung Ta that French patrols would be circulating incessantly throughout the sector and that they had received formal orders to fire on all military formations or groups of men, who could not give immediate proof that they were *bona fide* peasants going to or coming from their fields.

Activity within the Battalion itself was intense and we were all worn out by constant patrolling and guard duty. Everybody was nervy and trigger-happy and, with the standing order issued by Angeli, of which copies had been circulated at platoon level, we had little compunction about shooting down anybody who looked or acted suspiciously.

There was a sharp recrudescence of loot, rape and general terrorisation of the local peasantry, many of whom were either Caodai or Caodai sympathisers. Arrests were frequent and there was a definite upward trend in the number of Lieutenant Blairot's interrogations. Coupled with his normal sadism was the desire to get even with the Caodai who had complained bitterly and on more than one occasion of the looting of the Bande Noire.

After one particularly lucrative night-raiding patrol, with Estaing and his men, he had returned to the Bande Noire's section of the post with a herd of fifteen bullocks, a score of pigs, poultry galore and several oxcarts full of rice. The whole was rapidly sold for a handsome price and the results went into the Bande Noire's kitty after deduction of Lieutenant Blairot's share. The villagers from whom the livestock and produce had been taken came to Battalion HQ to reclaim their possessions. Blairot blandly announced that the livestock and paddy in question had been recovered from a renowned Viet stockhold and Colonel Angeli obligingly turned a blind eye to the affair, until he was certain that the livestock and produce in question had been disposed of, when, to calm the indignant villagers, he consented to search the Bande Noire compound. He found nothing and announced the fact to the villagers, adding that their cattle and rice must have been stolen by a Viet raiding party. The incident was closed to the satisfaction of everyone but the villagers. It had been a near squeak for Blairot, however, and he had neither forgotten nor forgiven.

Both Lieutenant Blairot and Colonel Angeli were due to leave Indochina, their turn of duty having come to an end. Shortly before leaving, Blairot indulged in what was perhaps the most crapulous and revolting of all his interrogations. (We had managed to force him to ease up a bit in his methods by pointing out that not only was his office in full view of the village but also that, on account of the noise he made, it was impossible to get any work done in the HQ buildings). In any case a prisoner who had witnessed the end of the affair in question, escaped the same night and, till the day he left for France, Blairot never dared leave the post without a heavily armed escort and by jeep. Estaing, who was due to leave a month after Blairot, was also extremely cautious about his movements. They were both indexed by the Viet and the story that the escaped prisoner had to tell was sure to put them at the top of the list for immediate liquidation. The Viet intelligence system was efficient and well-developed insofar as key European army personnel was concerned.

It was a particularly hot, damp and airless day and we were all tired and on edge owing to the climate and the Caodai troubles. A neighbouring post had sent in a couple of natives suspected of spying and had left them, hog-tied in Blairot's office, for questioning.

Blairot had gone off for a drink, and as there was no one in his office the NCO who had brought in the prisoners asked me to sign for them and to put a guard over them. A few minutes later the orderly, whom I had sent to watch the prisoners, came in to say that Blairot had arrived. His office was just next door so I went across to give him the papers the NCO had left. He read them, told me to wait and then went over to the prisoners, kicked them on to their backs and took a little walk over their bellies to get the dust off his shoes. When he had finished he sent an orderly up to the Bande Noire with orders to send along a dozen men, the two 'specialists' and an interpreter. The orderly gone, he turned to me and told me to stay and watch the proceedings. The Colonel was away for the day, I had nothing very important to do and, having heard Blairot at work for months, I was morbidly attracted by the idea of watching his methods. The results I had seen often enough to have been repelled by the idea, but curiosity got the better of me. I decided to watch it out.

Once they were all in the office he had the suspects untied and stretched out on to the floor face down—a man standing on each limb and another on the neck. When they were well in position and firmly held he started to beat them himself with everything that came into his hands, working himself into a frenzy of rage.

Even so, he managed to control his blows enough to ensure that they reached the kidneys.

As soon as he was exhausted he had the two men hauled to their knees, still firmly held by the Bande Noire, and told the interpreter to start questioning them. While they were being questioned he grabbed a metal ruler and kept up a steady back-hand fore-hand slashing across their throats, their heads being held back so that they could gain no protection from their chins. The men, speechless with agony, could do little more than whimper and gasp for air. They were too far gone even to understand the questions they were being asked. Furious at what he considered their stubbornness, Blairot had them stretched out on the floor again, backs to the ground, and ordered the two specialists to give them a liver and solar plexus massage. It took the five men holding each man all their strength to hold the two as they writhed and strained to break away from the torture.

Estaing, who had been called in to assist at the interrogation, left in disgust, knowing too well that neither would be capable of saying a word after the treatment they were receiving. He knew from experience the state into which Blairot was working himself up, and he wanted to have no part or parcel in the inevitable end of the session, which was bound to be as disgusting as it would be useless.

By that time a considerable crowd of sensation-mongers had gathered around Blairot's office door, which was wide open. Blairot, excited by the pleasure of the crowd, had the two men jerked to their feet and gave them a good working over with his fists. When he had finished with them they were little more than two shuddering lumps of tortured flesh, barely sensible and temporarily incapable of any further reaction to pain, pleasure, or life itself.

The whole performance had been accompanied by a flow of invective and abuse from Blairot, who ranted on in a desperate monologue about the dangerous character of his two victims. Once they had been reduced to impotence he had worked himself up to

G   97

such a pitch of excitement that he was incapable of letting the matter drop. After a short period of reflection he ordered the two suspects to be carried up to the prisoners' compound and put into the little cell, which stood isolated in one corner of the compound.

The compound itself was surrounded by barbed wire and was placed on a rising knoll of ground near the edge of the post and in full view of the street, which bordered the outer barbed-wire defences and earthworks. A series of broken-down old tents had been rigged up in the middle of the compound to give the prisoners a little shelter from the sun and the rains. For their drinking and washing water there was a disused well. The cell itself was used to isolate dangerous prisoners and for sessions of super-interrogation. While the two men were being carried to the cell, Blairot went off to another part of the post to fetch the war-dog. It was an Alsatian specially trained for use on patrols to sniff out ambushes and traps. However, it proved to be useless on patrol and was kept chained up in a kennel—too vicious to let loose and too highly strung for work. It had also been trained to attack natives but was incapable of distinguishing between the Viets and our auxiliaries and the results had been disastrous.

By the time that Blairot got back to the compound a crowd had gathered and was waiting to watch the developments of his interrogation. In spite of the heat and the midday meal which was ready, the men were eager for a sensation. The compound itself was full, the prisoners having been brought in from work and locked up for the siesta. Blairot strode arrogantly through the crowd and into the compound with the dog, on a short leash, at his heels. The prisoners scattered as he got into the compound. They were mortally afraid of the dog, who had already bitten more than one of them. Excited by the crowd, the unaccustomed walk and the sight and smell of the prisoners, the dog was slavering and straining at the leash in an effort to get at the latter.

Blairot let the dog excite itself for a while, then told the interpreter to go into the cell and tell the two men that if they didn't talk he would loose the dog on them. The interpreter came back and said that the men were incapable of talking and suggested that they be left alone until they had recovered sufficiently to make sense. Blairot, however, was past reasoning and was excited by the interrogation, the eager faces of the crowd and by the frightened mass of prisoners, who were huddled in a corner of the compound trying to attract as little attention as possible. Back into the cell went the interpreter, only to come out a few minutes later insisting that the two men were past the possibility of making any sense. They were too far gone, he said, to understand or to answer anything; it was useless to try to get anything out of them for at least twenty-four hours. Blairot was adamant. He insisted that they were shamming to gain time, that he had hardly touched them, but that now he would surely wake them up a bit and get them to talk. He pushed the interpreter to one side and took the dog up to the cell door, working it to a fever pitch of excitement with encouraging noises and commands. Once the dog had reached a point of slavering fury he slipped the leash, loosed it into the cell, where the two men lay with their hands bound tight behind their backs, and closed the door.

The men who were watching outside the compound stirred in pleasurable anticipation, the prisoners in the compound crouched even lower and were motionless; eyes distant and heads turned away from the cell, they trembled with a wave of compassion for the two men in the cell. Blairot grinning and swaggering, was strutting up and down before the cell door. For a moment after the dog went into the cell a hush fell over the assembly, broken a second later by the mad, bloodlust growling and worrying of the dog and the high screaming wails of blind terror and anguish from the men it was tearing to pieces. After two or three minutes the only sounds from the cell came from the dog and Blairot opened the door and went in. He came out, dragging the quivering blood-drenched animal on the end of the leash, and handed the leash over to the dog's keeper with the orders to take it back to the kennel and give it a good meal. He then turned round to the huddled mass of prisoners and, calling four of them over to him, ordered them to bring the two bodies out from the cell. Cowed, the prisoners obeyed and dragged out the broken corpses, placed them at Blairot's feet and waited.

Blairot laughed and told the interpreter to tell the prisoners to have a good look and to realise that it was far more healthy to answer questions when he was in charge of an interrogation. With that he strode off to lunch and the crowd broke up and followed his example.

During the siesta the compound prisoners washed out the cell, lifted the two bodies into the shade of the tents and covered them with palm leaves to keep the flies away. Later in the day the bodies were loaded on to a jeep and dumped in a paddy-field a few miles away. By the next morning they had disappeared, Estaing having verified the fact in the course of a patrol. That night one of the compound prisoners escaped and his escape passed unnoticed till the following morning.

During the whole of the compound session, natives passing along the street outside, curious about the unusual gathering around the prisoner compound, had stopped and waited to see what was going on. They didn't leave till the end of the proceedings. Though they could see nothing of what went on inside the cell, they had seen Blairot arrive with the dog, they had heard his very loud conversation with the interpreter— it had been carried on in French and those who understood French had translated for the others who didn't—above all, they had seen the dog go into the cell. They had heard the noise of the dog at work and the hopeless agony in the screams of the dying men, they had seen Blairot come out with the dog and later the prisoners carrying out the two bodies. When Blairot turned to leave the compound they scattered gravely and went on their respective ways to spread the news of what they had just witnessed.

Chapter

10

COUPLED WITH THE massive desertions of the Caodaist regulars to the dissenting army, April was marked by a sharp recrudescence of Viet road-mining, night attacks on small towers and terrorist killing of pro-French Annamites. As a direct result there was a corresponding increase in the number of French retaliatory patrols and actions which brought in an ever-swelling number of prisoners and suspects—a very satisfactory state of affairs for the Battalion. We had been obliged to undertake the construction of a considerable number of new watch-towers and small posts throughout the sector as well as the repairing of a number of the buildings at the HQ post and the construction of several dormitories. The work in hand would normally have meant employing an important gang of local civilian coolies, bricklayers and carpenters. With the influx of prisoners, however, the situation was considerably eased.

The old hands among the prisoners, who had learnt a little French and who could understand European ways, were all needed for operational purposes, their job being to carry reserve ammunition, radio posts, mortar shells and supplies; they could not be spared for the building work. The rank and file of the Battalion who were not in fit marching condition were kept at the post for guard and general security duties as well as for local patrols, and had but

The Post

little time or energy left for building. Native labour had to be paid for and the money came out of the funds allocated for the work in hand. With unlimited prisoner labour the situation was saved, the work could go ahead and there would be a handsome profit for the kitty at the end—added to which there was the money saved on the prisoners themselves. The State accorded a daily maintenance allowance for every prisoner declared and the money was handed over to the 2ème Bureau—Lieutenant

Blairot—which was charged with their upkeep. There was always a considerable rake-off for the kitty.

The prisoner system was an essential and vital part of Indochinese military life, in which the prisoners were indispensable for the everyday fatigue duties of sweeping, cleaning, water-hauling and kitchen help as well as for construction. The Légionnaires were too worn out by the climate, incessant patrol and operational activity, internal security duties and alcohol to have any energy left for the chores. As a result every post and unit kept a quota of prisoners to ease the burden of the fighting troops. Few of the prisoners were *bona fide* prisoners of war; the latter were normally sent back to Base headquarters, where they were screened for political re-education and ultimate inclusion in the ranks of the newly-formed Bao Dai army.

The prisoners kept in the posts were natives picked up as suspected Viet agents, possible saboteurs, suppliers of material to the Viet, local criminals who had been sentenced, or unfortunates who had just happened to be around at the wrong moment and had been picked up by a passing patrol. Periodically a commission of prisoner controllers came round to check up on the prisoners held, revise old sentences and decide on the fate of new arrivals. The commissioners were appointed by the Bao Dai Government in Saigon. Both military and civilian intelligence and legal bodies were represented. It was a sane and efficient system which gave the prisoners the satisfaction of knowing for how long they were going to be held.

There was, however, another category of prisoners—'black market' prisoners who were held by the army and hidden or dispatched elsewhere every time the control commission came around. In the main they were men and women against whom nothing definite could be proved and who would have been released by the commission. They included personal enemies of the Bande Noire and their imprisonment was both arbitrary and illegal. They never figured on any official list and no maintenance allowance was received for their upkeep, which mattered but little as they were fed from the surplus stock of supplies looted by the Bande Noire. The length of imprisonment for these prisoners was unpredictable and depended on the personal whim of Estaing, Blairot, Angeli, or, in other units, on that of the unit commander. It ranged from days to years and, when liberated, the prisoners were sufficiently aware of what would happen to them if they made an official complaint and ever fell into army hands again to keep their mouths shut.

The 'black market' prisoner was an especially valuable combat commodity for, if he got killed on operations whilst serving as bearer, there were no complications and no official reports to be made, no relations to inform; he was just left dead on the terrain and was usually listed as 'enemy killed in action'. All of which was common practice and common knowledge and, though frowned upon officially, received unofficial benediction. The only people to suffer were the natives unfortunate enough or simple to let themselves be taken in for questioning.

Another advantage of the 'black market' prisoner was the cash he brought in. For construction, road-building and brush-clearing jobs the battalion received fixed credits which included the sums estimated necessary for the payment of local labour employed. Since the overwhelming majority of the coolies were illiterate, the pay-roll receipts were countersigned with Xs. Instead of calling in local labour the 'black market' prisoners were put to work and a moderately intelligent clerk was assigned the job of making out a pay-roll. All he had to do was to mark Xs against imaginary names with as many variations on the Xs as he could devise. The profits went into the kitty of the unit in-volved, whether commando, company or battalion and when the Quartermaster-General came round to control the work done and the use of the credits allocated, he was always content—the work was done, the credits fully spent and the pay-roll none too neatly countersigned by an unquestionably variegated row of Xs.

The same system was employed in so far as the auxiliairy troops were concerned. Administratively, for the sector, they all came under the control of Lieutenant Le Tourneau whether they served in the commandos or in the auxiliary company responsible for manning the road watch-towers. It was Le Tourneau who drove down to Saigon every month, collected the pay for the men listed on the nominative control and paid them. There again it was customary to declare all the men illiterate and to countersign with Xs, but Le Tourneau's problem was slightly more complicated—he had to pay the men.

However, he had hit on a very simple solution. When an auxiliary was killed, and providing the death had been moderately discreet, it was not declared for several months. Le Tourneau pocketed the dead man's pay and the only loser was the state. A big beefy character with twenty-odd years of service, he had come up through the ranks and knew all the ropes well enough to stay within the safety limit. He was a cheerful, open-handed, hearty drinker who managed to put his pay to one side every month and to get by on what he could fiddle, spending most of that in Thieu's or in the mess. When sober he was reasonably good company, and Blanchet and I spent many an evening drinking and chatting with him in the resort for 'better-class people'. We had finally converted it into a kind of unofficial club, and there, with Thieu's connivance, we usually managed to freeze out any undesirable who happened to stray in for a drink. It was a cosy arrangement and used by Blanchet, Le Tourneau, Estaing and myself as well as one or two other kindred spirits including Lieutenant Dindon, the Battalion Treasurer, who was a delightful if somewhat drunken incompetent; he had started life as a policeman and had wound up as the senior Lieutenant of the French army, seemingly unlikely ever to achieve his captaincy—not surprising, considering he had left the police force as he had been incapable of passing from constable to the next rank.

By then, I had been promoted to Lance-Sergeant, and was waiting to be promoted to Sergeant. I had fully taken over Tranchant's job of temporary-acting unpaid Battalion

Sergeant-Major, he having been repatriated. Thieu was delighted by our use of his place. He seemed to feel that it guaranteed his security and future business possibilities. After all, Blanchet was the Police Commissioner, Le Tourneau was in charge of the auxiliaries and their supplies, Dindon was Battalion Treasurer, Estaing was the boss of the Bande Noire and disposed of their loot, and I was the rather shaky right hand of the battalion and sector commander—all small fry but capable of hooking big fish. From our point of view it was an eminently satisfactory situation—the place was comfortable and discreet, we could say what we liked and Thieu was so eager to do business that rounds on the house abounded and odd side-dishes of local delicacies poured out of his kitchen and on to our table in a steady and succulent stream.

A couple of days after Blairot had called in the war-dog to question suspects, Blanchet and I strolled down to Thieu's where we found Estaing and Le Tourneau already installed and apparently on their third or fourth round. They were busy discussing the efficacy of the Viet information services and local terrorists and propaganda groups. Estaing, who knew better than most of us, insisted that we were all living in a glass-house and that most of what we did, said or even thought was known and noted down; adding that the Viet maintained a first-class filing system in which were included not only Europeans renowned for brutality but also the officers, NCOs and men who worked in key positions. They obtained their information by devious means and their filing system was kept up to date.

The informers were found amongst the congaies, mess boys, auxiliaries and even the men of the Bande Noire, of whom many were renegade Viets and amongst whom there were certainly one or two acting as double agents. Stopping the flow of information would be, he said, like trying to bail out a sinking boat with a sieve. The French were justly and universally unpopular and nearly every native was willing to pass on to the Viet the slightest piece of information, no matter how unimportant. The Viet knew the weaknesses and failings of the majority of officers and NCOs, be it drink, women, opium, boys or gambling, and once certain of a man's vice, they would wait patiently for the opportune moment to help the vice and the downward trend. It was a very subtle and insidious form of sabotage which had on many occasions proved successful, bringing about the complete downfall or death of the man involved, which in turn meant that he had to be replaced and automatically caused a corresponding loss in time and efficiency all round.

The majority of that kind of indirect sabotage was entrusted to an organisation known as the Dich Van. The Dich Van agents went through a long and complicated training before being sent off on a mission and, as in most Viet organisations, worked in groups of three. One member specialised in the spreading of anti-French propaganda and at the same time acted as recruiting agent for the Viet regular and regional armies. The second concentrated on contacting European and auxiliary troops to obtain information and undermine morale. The third acted as liaison agent between the group and headquarters and contacted local agents. The role of second agent was frequently given to women: clever and attractive physically, by European standards, they tried to become either the congaies of European soldiers or else the wives of auxiliaries. In either case they were hard to spot before the damage was done, by which time they had usually disappeared with their mission accomplished.

Even when caught it was rare that a Dich Van agent talked; they were all fanatical supporters of Ho Chi Minh and on the rare occasions when they had broken under torture the information they had given turned out to be false. The liaison agent, when not travelling, spent most of his time hanging round markets and cafés frequented by soldiers listening to what was said and piecing together the odd scraps of information. The Europeans as a whole were shockingly indiscreet and carried on conversations about past and future operations as though the Viet had never thought of sending out agents who were trained linguists.

All of which sounded pretty depressing and exaggerated, and Blanchet and I said so, adding that Estaing was just being bloody-minded on account of Blairot's recent session. Le Tourneau, however, backed him up and added that he had the devil's own job with his auxiliaries. To begin with they received starvation wages, they held a grudge against the French who treated them like dirt, even when they were NCOs or commissioned officers, and left them to defend under-armed and virtually undefendable watch-towers, without any means of communication other than Verey lights in the case of attack.

The Dich Van propaganda was ideally suited to influence them and it was not infrequent to find a post abandoned, the men having cleared out with arms, belongings and womenfolk. It nearly always turned out that one of the auxiliaries had married a Dich Van agent who had, after several weeks of persuasion, organised the desertion by promising rewards and better conditions on the Viet side. In other cases the men in the watch-towers let Viet columns and supplies go by without taking any action, in exchange for a little cash and a promise from the Viets to leave them off the lists of towers to be attacked. Sometimes they even sold munitions to the Viet, and frequently, when French patrols were out at night and passed the towers, they would fire a warning shot to give the local Viets time to disappear.

It was virtually impossible to check or prevent this state of affairs as the rot had gone far too deep. Occasional controls and radical changes of personnel introduced a temporary lull, but lost time was soon made up and things went on as before. Le Tourneau accepted the fact as a fact and considered himself lucky to get by with so little trouble. At least desertions were fairly isolated and enough towers repelled attacks to offset attention to those which had succumbed.

He went on to add that 'cowardice' and 'treachery' were terms easy enough to employ, but they were practically inapplicable to the auxiliaries. The Annamites had frequently proved themselves as loyal and courageous as any European, if not more so, but they felt they were getting a raw deal and saw no point in heroics. Given an ideal and suitable leadership they would go anywhere and against anything. The trouble, as he saw it, lay in the fact that the quality of the European officers and NCOs designated to command the native troops was abysmally low. The European habits of drink, copulation and graft left them wide open to Viet propaganda and impaired their faculties of judgment and reflex. All too frequently auxiliaries were hit, kicked and generally roughed around by their European commanders, and in each case it left behind a violent and lasting resentment which was easily turned to active hatred.

By the time that Le Tourneau had finished it was getting late, so Blanchet, Estaing and I left—we had to get back to the mess to eat. On the way back, Estaing, who still had something on his mind, started off again on the subject of those indexed by the Viet—this time he started to talk about Nielsen.

Nielsen was the wonder-boy of the Battalion. At twenty-three, after only two years in Indochina, he had piled up nine Croix de Guerre, the Military Medal (highest French decoration for the rank and file); an arm smashed up by an explosive bullet, the rank of Lance-Sergeant in the field, and still he wanted more. He was a specialist at pulling off spectacular one-man raids against the Viet and had shot down more of them than anyone in the battalion. Estaing was convinced that the Viet would get him— he took too many risks and he had taken to drinking to keep his nerves steady. Once that started the end was in sight; alcohol played hell with a man's reactions.

On that gloomy note Estaing left us to have another drink. He didn't feel like eating.

Estaing must have had double sight. Nielsen went out on patrol the next day and was killed in an ambush with six of the ten men who were with him. Three others were wounded. It shook all of us who had known him well; he had become the battalion mascot. I had always liked him; he had a strange quality of sensibility mixed with his buccaneering propensities which made him a very good companion.

When he came out of hospital with a semi-paralysed arm (result of a bullet through the elbow while he was cleaning up a Viet stronghold) he took to drinking in earnest. Every time he went out his brandy-flask went along with him and if he didn't go off on a night patrol or ambush he stayed in his room mopping it up. Not that he got drunk; his nerves were all shot to hell and if he didn't kill at least one man a day he had to drink. If, during the day, he found nothing he went off by himself at night and prowled around the neighbouring cainhas till he heard voices. Then he would burst in, bump off the inhabitants and go back to bed feeling better. But our post was badly situated for that and there were few cainhas inhabited in the vicinity—the majority of the natives had withdrawn to the woods or their underground hideouts—and often he would come back with the jitters and drink till he felt calmer.

For over a year he had felt that he had passed the point of no return. At first Indochina had been a sport. He went out on patrol and his luck always held good—frequently he bagged a Viet or two and often managed to bring in odd weapons and documents. From time to time he pulled off a particularly spectacular *coup de main* with his group and was awarded another Croix de Guerre or a promotion. Each time it meant drinks all round and a general celebration. Slowly and surely the drinks became a necessity, until he reached the point where he had to take a bottle along with him every time he went out, in case he got the jitters. Then he found that the remedy for alcohol was blood, and to forget the blood, alcohol. On the rare occasions he was really sober, disgust settled down in a glutinous huddle on his head and he realised that he was finished; he could never leave Indochina alive, he could no longer face the idea of going home. The only things left were alcohol and going out to kill Annamites —whether Vietminh or Vietnam it was of no importance, they all stank anyway, alive or dead.

We got the full story from Pagliocco, sole untouched survivor of the ambush, later in the day.

Nielsen had gone into the platoon hut at dawn and rooted his two groups out of their beds, telling them to get ready for a patrol. The men grumbled; they had been out most of the night on an ambush and all the day before on patrol. They wanted to rest up a bit. But with Nielsen there was never any rest—he seemed to think of nothing but going out Viet-hunting.

The older hands in the group didn't like it—the way they looked at it, one man's glory inevitably meant somebody else stopping a packet.

Sullenly enough two depleted groups of the platoon lined up and they started off, ten strong, down the track which Nielsen always took. He was in the lead with two scouts, the others following at five-pace intervals. Nielsen was so confident in his flair for smelling out Viet trouble that he never bothered to change his itinerary or spread his men out further. They had followed the brush-bordered track for about fifteen hundred yards when it came.

It came in the form of half a dozen 80-millimetre mortar shells, laid as mines and fired off by remote control, backed up by a heavy fire of automatic weapons. Nielsen, the two scouts, the two group corporals and two other men went down either dead or dying—three others, badly wounded, were out for the count. Private Pagliocco grabbed up the Bren and magazine case from a man who had gone down in front of him, and dived into a shallow ditch to one side of the track.

He realised instinctively that the Viet would close in to get the weapons of the men lying on the track and to finish off the wounded, if any were still alive. He fired off the first charger in quick bursts, aiming low on both sides of the track. Watching and listening intently, he let rip a burst every time he saw a leaf stir or heard a rustle. He didn't know exactly where the Viets were, but he sensed that they were closing in and then he saw something that made him realise they were closer than he had thought.

III

About fifteen yards ahead of him he saw Corporal Weiss, whom he had thought dead, wobble a revolver up to his head and fire. The first shot missed, and he fired again and made it. Pagliocco had seen that Weiss's jaw had been blown off and that his belly had been ripped open—he must have seen the Viets getting near to him and blown his brains out to avoid being beheaded.

Pagliocco went a little berserk; he got to his knees and let rip with three chargers in the direction Weiss must have been looking and then another two for good measure spraying another side of the track. He began to realise that it was a matter of yards, minutes and ammunition. He seemed to have pinned the Viets down about ten yards from Nielsen and the two scouts, but he only had three chargers left and nobody seemed to be coming to the rescue—even though they must have heard the firing back at the post and realised that something had gone wrong.

He was down to his last charger and feeling pretty low when he heard a whistle blast, followed by sustained bursts of automatic fire coming from behind him. He saw a few Viets flitting off through the brush and loosed off the rest of his charger at them before getting to his feet. Before the rescue party could reach him, Pagliocco stopped them and made a quick and careful search. He found and neutralised four other mortar shells which hadn't gone off.

Chapter

I I

B Y APRIL I had got into the swing of my new job and
become accustomed to the increased tempo of work and
responsibilities. I found that I was pretty much my own master,
in the sense that I could take a day off when I felt like it or judged
it possible. From being an obscure corporal I had not only
mounted in rank but suddenly found myself in control of the
administrative life of the Battalion.

Within a very short time I realised that, if my personal popu-
larity had not increased, at least I was consistently sought after
by officers and NCOs of other companies to help them iron out
odd difficulties before the Battalion Commander got to know
of them. In this way I had managed, on one or two occasions,
to help Captain Blanche. He had only just arrived from France
and there were quite a number of routine problems which he ran
foul of to begin with. I had straightened things out for him
several times when he asked me if I wouldn't care to switch to
his company. I was all for the idea and asked him to press the
matter with the Battalion Commander. The latter agreed to
let me go once my relief had come out from Africa. It was four
months before he arrived, but I got my transfer in the end.
The idea delighted me because Sergeant Hartz, a good friend of
mine, was in C Company, which was in any case about the best

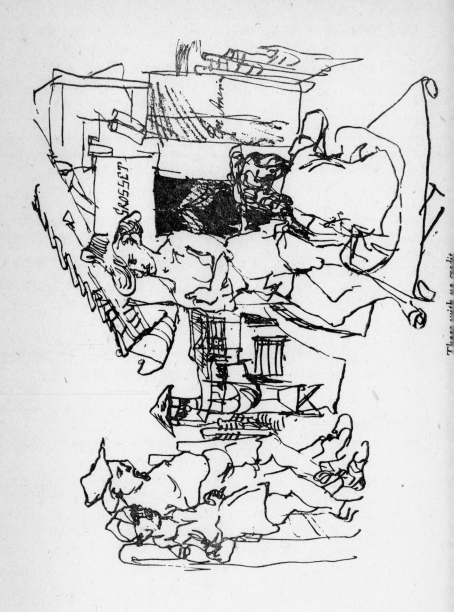

of the Regiment, and I was in the habit of dropping over to lunch with him on Sunday if I was free. The second Sunday in April I thumbed a ride to the village of Cay Chi, C Company's base. It was a Sunday no different to many others—the dead heat of the late morning sun had driven most of the human life under shelter. The only visible signs of it when I arrived at the post was a sentry dozing at the entrance and another sitting up in the watch-tower staring into space with sweaty inattention. The rank and file of C Company were off duty for the day and mostly were in town, having showered and changed into clean clothes, after the routine everyday chores of road-opening and security patrols.

Inside the buildings, however, there was a hum of activity. The cooks and their native prisoner helpers were putting the finishing touches to the Sunday lunch. In the men's canteen those who still had credit were trying to drown their thirst with local beer; in the sergeants' mess Hartz, another guest and myself and the three locally unmarried NCOs were piling down our pre-lunch short drinks and noisily discussing the doings of the week. Before going to the mess I had paid a courtesy visit to Captain Blanche and had been invited to drink a glass of champagne with the local Planter and his congaie who were lunching in his bungalow. Officer-NCO relationships were very elastic. It would have been a serious breach of etiquette had I not presented myself and had he not offered me a drink. I was just in time to finish the second bottle. He had given me another to take over to the mess and our shorts were champagne cocktails.

In the village, which surrounded the post on three sides, the Chinese and Annamite pubs were doing a roaring trade with those who hadn't any credit left in the company canteen—the prices were double, but what the hell, it went on the slate. It was even Sunday for the Viet and local prisoners whose families had been let into the prison compound for the day, after a thorough search for propaganda and hidden weapons.

Gradually the morning disintegrated and the afternoon

pattern began to form under the constantly increasing weight of the heat. In the sergeants' mess Smedlow, Rossini and Moineau were indulging in their usual Sunday after-lunch fight, plates flying, bottles breaking and the Annamite boy screaming like a stuck pig just for the fun of it. Hartz and I sipped our brandy and ducked the flying crockery. A few huts away, in the village, we could hear Sergeant de Perre quietly and methodically beating up his congaie, who was crying on a soft, penetrating, brain-piercing note. From the Captain's bungalow we could hear the Captain explaining to the Planter's congaie how much he was loved by his men and admired by his superiors—the Planter was undoubtedly snoozing over his after-lunch brandy. In the men's quarters the few who were either too broke or too tired to be in town snored and sweated their way through the siesta. The sentries at the gate and up in the watch-tower were far away in their native Würtemburg or Calabria. It was just another Sunday no different to many others.

Apart from the quiet sibilant cackle of the villagers the residual hum of vocal noise was basically teutonic. Gradually, in between fly-bites, Hartz and I were sinking deeper and deeper into an after-lunch state of torpor. The few beers and the brandy or two we had drunk in the mess had helped to lull us to sleep. The whole post reeked of dampness—our clothes were drenched—the flies had definitely finished their siesta and had turned to with voracity, and the stench of stale heat made breathing difficult.

Hartz and I had been dozing away for a few minutes, stretched out in deck-chairs with our feet up, when Sergeant de Perre came in. Finished with his wife-beating for the day, he wanted a drink, but not alone. He woke us up and insisted on paying for a round. It was too much effort to refuse so we accepted. We chatted about this and that for a few minutes, in a desultory fashion, then de Perre suddenly suggested that we ought to borrow the Planter's jeep and run up to the Commando Post at Cau Xoi. It was only a ten-minute run, we could have a drink there and be back within half an hour. Anything was better than sitting and stewing so we agreed readily enough. He went off to ask the Planter's permission. The Planter had always been very friendly with the Company and, if he wasn't using his jeep, lent it willingly. He didn't even say anything if someone borrowed it for a short spin without having asked him first.

It was with some surprise, therefore, that we saw the Planter and de Perre come charging into the mess with the news that the jeep had gone. Hartz and I tried to keep the Planter cooled down with a drink while de Perre went off to investigate. The Planter had woken up with an after-lunch hangover and was hard to handle. Finally de Perre came back with the news that the jeep had been taken by Schroeder, the Captain's ex-chauffeur who had been fired for drinking, and Klein, a friend of his. The sentry at the gate had seen them disappear in the direction of Saigon and thinking they were on official business hadn't bothered to stop them. After a hurried discussion as to what should be done it was decided that the Captain ought to be warned. We left that to the Planter.

The Sunday calm was shattered by a roar from the Captain—champagne, lunch, brandy and the heat all helped to work up his rage. Pandemonium reigned for a few minutes—the odd NCOs and the men in the Post, awakened by the noise, were straggling out of the different buildings. The Captain was shouting that he wouldn't have deserters in *his* company . . . he's shoot them . . . beat them up . . . send them to prison. . . .

Goggle-eyed with wonder, the men stood around waiting to see what would happen—most of them had slipped off to Saigon for an afternoon and some even in a 'borrowed' car. The Captain, realising that he had an audience, simmered down and gave orders that the Dodge truck was to be ready with a fully-armed combat group aboard within five minutes. With that he turned and disappeared into his bungalow, followed by the Planter. The men shrugged their shoulders and shuffled off while the duty-sergeant detailed the combat group. Five minutes later the Dodge and the combat group were ready and the Captain hurried out of his bungalow, jumped in next to the driver and gave the order to drive to Saigon as fast as the truck would go.

The rest of the story I got from Hartz, who had gone with the Captain, and from the police report I received in the office a few days later. It was only a beginning to the series of bad-luck stories which were to hit C Company during the next few weeks.

Schroeder and Klein had passed the control-post at Baqueo, on the outskirts of Saigon, without any trouble—they told the MP that they had to go and fetch their CO in the Planter's jeep, the other having broken down. The MP didn't even notice the carbine they had 'borrowed' before leaving the post, ostensibly in case they ran into trouble with the Viet.

Schroeder drove straight on towards Saigon until they saw a quiet cul-de-sac where they could change. Dressed as they were in uniform and without a pass they would certainly get into trouble with the MPs inside Saigon; so they had taken the pre-caution of bringing along civilian clothes. They stopped, changed, and wrapping the carbine up in their discarded army rigs, stowed the bundle in the back of the jeep and went on down to Saigon to spend the few hundred piastres left over from their last pay.

The Dodge bucked and roared its way towards Saigon. The driver was in a muck sweat by the time they drew up at the Baqueo control-post, the road had never been built to take trucks at that speed and it was as much through luck as skill that he had avoided countless plunges into the bordering paddy-fields. They stopped at the control long enough to check on the jeep's passage and to send off a message to the Provost-Marshal that it was to be stopped and the occupants arrested. The Captain refused to leave the group's armament at the post as required. To avoid trouble in the town there was a standing order that with-out special permission all armament should be left at the control-posts. He insisted that he was chasing armed deserters and, sweeping aside the objections of the MP, jumped back into the truck and roared off towards Saigon. Once in the city, he directed the driver into the main boulevards and told him to cruise around them, slowly, to see if they would pick up the jeep.

Up and down they went through the crowded Sunday streets, almost too jammed to move. Suddenly from the back of the truck came a resounding view-halloo; the men had spotted the jeep crossing an intersection they had just passed. The driver whipped his truck round, heedless of the other traffic, and shot off in pursuit. By skilful driving he brought them up to within two car-lengths of the jeep.

Schroeder and Klein, dressed in civilian clothes, were driving calmly along looking at the Sunday crowds and the girls. The Captain told the driver to try to squeeze the jeep against the sidewalk and warned the men behind not to make any noise. A sudden opening in the traffic ahead allowed the Dodge to slide up on the tail of the jeep. Klein turned his head at the same moment, saw the Dodge, the Captain, the armed men and hurriedly told Schroeder who, slamming down the accelerator, shot ahead and turned into a one-way street. The jeep danced up the street scattering bicycles, *pousse-pousses* and stalls as it went, with the Dodge in hot pursuit putting the finishing touches to the chaos started by the jeep. To add to the general confusion and racket the Captain, who realised that the jeep would give him the slip, ordered the men to fire a warning burst in the air—for the men, excited by the chase, this was too good to be true. Their copious warning bursts sprayed the walls, the pavements, the street, the air and, it was later discovered, the jeep.

Meanwhile, terrorised passers-by were leaping for shelter in all direction before the triple menace of the jeep, the Dodge and the ricocheting bullets. Taking advantage of the general panic Schroeder, by then thoroughly rattled, managed to slip into another sidestreet and disappear. The jeep was found later that night abandoned and bullet-ridden, in a back alley a considerable distance from the scene of pursuit.

After a further and fruitless search the Captain headed for the

Provost-Marshal's office. Still excited by the chase, he strode into the building full of his story, followed by Hartz. A few minutes later he came out a considerably chastened man after a full-powered 'Who the hell do you think you are, a piddling little Captain, to conduct a Wild West chase through the streets of Saigon—armed troops in Saigon indeed . . . I don't care if your wholy bloody Company has deserted and stolen a plantation full of jeeps . . . After one look at you it wouldn't surprise me. . . . Good God, man, I'll have you busted for this . . . Now get out of here while I try to clear up this mess and don't move until you are told to. . . .'

Schroeder and Klein found a quiet alley and, thoroughly shaken, parked the jeep and got out. They had started off on foot when Schroeder remembered the carbine, went back, scooped up the bundle and hurriedly rejoined Klein.

Of the two, Klein was in the worse shape and though neither had been touched by the bullets their nerves were shot to pieces. Schroeder took command and telling Klein to stick close and follow he set off towards a Chinese bath-house where he knew the proprietor. After a ten-minute walk they reached it, a frowsy-looking place in a dirty dilapidated back street. Without bothering to knock, he pushed open the door and walked in. Klein followed, sat down in a rickety bamboo chair and waited. Schroeder had gone on through a second door.

After a few minutes Schroeder came back with a bottle of beer and a screwdriver, handing the beer to Klein he began to dismantle the carbine; as soon as he had finished he hung the barrel down one trouser-leg, the stock down the other, and gave the odd bits to Klein who put them inside his shirt. Once the car-bine had disappeared, Schroeder went to the door and called out to someone. The man, a half-caste, who came in seemed to know Schroeder well and the two of them started to talk. Klein, who was still in a daze from the chase, took but little notice of and no part in the conversation. Finally Schroeder turned around, introduced him to the man as a friend of his and added for Klein's benefit that they were fixed up with a hotel for the night and that they had better be going.

Once out in the street, Schroeder explained that he had told the man that they were on leave, had lost all their money and didn't know where to go for the night—the man, who knew him fairly well, had rung up an hotel where there was a room at their disposal. The hotel wasn't far away and once there Schroeder went to the desk explained who they were and went straight up to the room without waiting to fill in the register. It was a terrible room, dark and evil-smelling, first-floor, and overlooked a squalid garbage-choked yard.

By this time Klein was really beginning to go to pieces; nothing made any sense any more and all he wanted and ached for was security. He tried to say as much to Schroeder but all he got was a grunt for an answer. Schroeder, who had kept the screwdriver, was sitting on the bed reassembling the carbine. Once he got it in working order he pushed in a charger and, turning to Klein, told him that after what had happened they would have to try to find a ship the next day. There was no question of going back to the Company, and he added that they were safe for the night; no one would be able to find them. When Klein asked why he had reassembled the gun he just muttered 'in case', then flung himself on the bed furthest from the door and went to sleep. Klein lay on the other bed in sweaty confusion, unable to think coherently and tortured by his inability to react. Finally he dozed off into a series of appalling nightmares.

The proprietor of the hotel and his wife, who were Chinese and no fools, hadn't liked the look of the two men. They were too nervous, in too much of a hurry to go up without signing the register, and the wife, who had crept up to listen at their door had heard a strange clicking noise which could have come from a gun of some kind. After a long discussion they decided that even though the bath-house proprietor was a friend of theirs it would be wiser to give the police a ring and ask them to drop round to verify the identity of their odd-looking customers.

If all was in order it could be passed off as a simple routine check; if not, the police would get the credit for the arrest, the hotel would be in the clear and there might even be a reward.

Klein woke with a start. He wasn't sure if it had been a part of his nightmare or if it had been a knock on the door and a summons to open in the name of the law. At the second knock, naked and trembling with fear he reached over to wake Schroeder and told him that the police were at the door. Schroeder, suddenly wideawake, muttered an oath, grabbed the carbine and, muttering that he had gone too far to be taken, rolled over towards the wall. Panic-stricken Klein leapt for the door and tried to open it—at that moment a shot rang out and the door burst open. The police found Klein a huddled whimpering wreck on the floor—on the bed furthest from the door lay Schroeder, the carbine clasped in his hands, his brains spattered over the bed.

As a result of the Captain's snap decision to conduct a man-hunt three coolies were in hospital suffering multiple fractures, Schroeder was dead and Klein had all the time in the world to regret his Sunday as he awaited trial on a pyramid of charges. The Captain's being censured was regarded as a tiresome misunderstanding on the part of his superiors.

Chapter

12

SHORTLY AFTER the incident of the man-hunt, Colonel Angeli, Lieutenant Blairot and a contingent of NCOs and other ranks nearly a hundred strong left for France. The new Battalion Commander, a Captain, was a man of a completely different stamp and soon enough the Companies began to feel the change. Where Angeli had been a bluff hard-hitting Viet-hunter with but little care for the finer shades of meaning of pacification, the new CO insisted that pacification meant what it said. Under Colonel Angeli's command the order of the day had been shoot first and ask afterwards and he had left behind a tough hard-hitting unit, which rarely bothered to ask any questions even afterwards. The new CO stressed the rights of the natives and forbade indiscriminate shooting. The 2ème Bureau had been run by Lieutenant Blairot according to Colonel Angeli's ideas. His successor, Lieutenant Draget, was in every possible way different and there too the change was evident within a very few days. Courage, ordinary everyday courage, of the kind that got men through the routine actions and ambushes, was of such common and normal occurrence that it mostly passed by without notice, being accepted as a normal part of a man's equipment—an integral part of the ordinary soldier and varied but slightly with the individual, much like the way he wore his hat or carried his gun.

From time to time there were rare and isolated incidents, such as Pagliocco's stand when the rest of the patrol was dead or wounded and his action stood out in relief against the behaviour of the others, or else a deed carried out with panache and bravura in the heat of an action as when Bouchard stood up with his Bren and solemnly sprayed a battalion of Viets who were advancing on his company at the double with a bugler sounding the charge —he bust the attack single-handed and without getting so much as a scratch.

Lieutenant Draget, however, had another kind of courage grafted into the everyday one of necessity. A cool steely quality, hard to perceive and deceptively inconspicuous. At first sight he was a weedy, palefaced bespectacled man of middle height and generally a very average specimen of humanity. He looked as though he would have been much happier if he had been left behind in some French garrison town as remount officer or town-major's clerk. When he arrived at the Battalion there were few of us who had known him before and only one who knew his story and it took quite a while for the men to realise that they had been allotted a full-blooded tiger. He had come in to take over the handling of the Bande Noire and his first action was to issue an order to all companies that all suspects and prisoners were to be handed over to him for questioning and in good condition, stressing that all unnecessary brutality would be heavily penalized.

Naturally enough a howl went up from the companies, who wanted to know who the hell he was to poke his nose into their affairs. They soon found out. Draget stolidly refused to use physical force during his questionings, maintaining that he would get as much, if not more, information by using straight psychological means. But to kick off with he had to fight a system which had had over four years in which to take root and flourish and he was up against a solid wall of opposition.

Shortly after his arrival he paid a courtesy call to each of the companies and commandos and at the same time had a look into their prisoner and intelligence systems. Where he saw things he thought needed changing—living conditions for prisoners, strong-arm methods to make them talk or an overabundance of prisoners declared as having been shot while trying to escape— he said so quietly and firmly. On account of his quietness the general impression was that he was a soft and ineffectual character and that it was pointless to take any notice of his orders which seemed more like suggestions than commands.

He even went so far as to forbid the stealing of suspects' effects and the raiding of cainhas by patrols as well as the finishing off of wounded natives who were usually killed and left lying. He maintained that it was bad propaganda and that the news would get around very fast that the wounded were being brought in and taken care of, which would have the direct effect of increasing the number of Viets rallying to the French. However, to explain all that and make it understood and put into practice took time, patience and almost Christlike forbearance.

Draget, a Belgian, had joined the Legion in the early days of 1939, his country had been swamped by the Germans and he thought it the best thing to do. During the war years he went through all the major campaigns—Norway, Egypt, North Africa, Syria, Italy, France, Germany, Middle East and in 1946 Indochina. In his first seven years of service he had amassed seven Croix de Guerre, the Military Medal, the Legion of Honour, and a fist full of British, American and Norwegian decorations, he had gone through every rank from private to second-lieutenant, most of his promotions being on the field and ratified later when he was due to go up one higher. He had come through the whole performance without a single wound and in seven years had had three weeks leave.

He stayed three years in Indochina the first time and picked up a further three Croix de Guerre without getting wounded— even though he had spent the entire time out in the brush, the jungle or the paddy-fields. When he came back to Indochina in 1952 he was a full Lieutenant and well on the way to being promoted Captain within a very short while and soon picked up yet another two Croix de Guerre. In the course of his career he had been naturalised French and married, though he rarely saw his wife or children.

Quiet, efficient and utterly conscious of what he was doing, he seemed to take things as they came and let time slide by. In fact he was vitally aware of everything that he did and said and rarely wasted a word or gesture. He knew well enough what was being said about him and the animosity that his new methods aroused —also that he was sharply criticised by a number of company commanders who treated him as though he had become an officer by accident. Quietly and firmly he insisted on his point of view and carried on with his work.

The first real shock came about two weeks after his appointment. All available officers and NCOs in the Battalion were summoned to be present outside HQ in parade dress and full decorations to welcome a visiting General. Draget took a discreet place at the end of the line of junior officers and was scarcely noticed by the assembled crowd of heroes and blood-thirsty Viet-hunters, who were busy indulging in an orgy of backslapping, handshaking and exchanging of the latest news from their respective areas.

There was a sudden flurry as the General's car hove in sight and we all drew up to attention. The General got out of his car, saluted us all courteously, saw Draget and with a beaming smile drew him out of the ranks and went off for a little stroll with him, chatting and laughing all the while. A slap on the back, a 'now-be-off-with-you-you-old-scoundrel' and the General rejoined the Battalion Commander and they made their way to the mess. The other officers, goggle-eyed with wonder, gathered round Draget and wanted to know what the General had said. 'Oh, nothing', we heard him say. 'We spent a couple of years together early on in the war and were just talking about old times.'

It was a very thoughtful group of men who went away to their companies to mull over Draget's influential friend. They had even had time to notice that his chest was loaded and that there was not a single wound star in the whole lot.

Slowly but surely he managed to straighten out the mess that Blairot had left behind and got the paper-work part of his job in order. At the same time the Bande Noire was reorganised so subtly that at first the men were unaware that any change had taken place, and by the time that they woke up to the fact that the more lucrative of their various rackets had been curbed and that they were going out on patrols without bringing back any loot it was too late to protest. A few got bloody-minded about the new conditions but the majority were enthusiastic supporters of Draget who, unlike Blairot, had eliminated all Europeans from the Bande Noire excepting himself and went out with them nearly every night—not on vague punitive expeditions but on ambushes and patrols acting on information which they had garnered. The results were good, though not conspicuous, and it was rare when they returned without having intercepted or captured the Viets or Viet informers they were after.

To top it all, Draget was no death-or-glory boy. He took calculated risks but refused to indulge in heroics and the newly inspired activities of the Bande Noire took them through the length and breadth of the sector. In a very short time they became the crack combat team in the Battalion and took immense pride in their achievements. At the same time he organised spy teams of two or three, choosing the surest of the men, and sent them off into Viet sectors to collect information. This game of carrying the war into the enemy camp delighted the men and they took an almost childish pride in rivalling each other's exploits.

Within six months Draget had changed the Bande Noire from a gang of thugs into a first-class information unit and the few exceptions who lamented the good old days and still indulged in isolated acts of murder, raping, etc., got short shrift from their fellows. At first the new tactics met with general mockery.

Draget was not a very martial figure and looked like a little spinster when he led his men out of an evening, in battledress and a brush hat pulled down over his ears, spectacles balanced on the end of his nose. He looked even more lamentable when he came back in the morning, soaked, muddy and worn out, the Bande Noire following leading a prisoner or two—the prisoners far fresher than he. His polite and gentle manner of interrogation seemed ludicrous after the performances of Blairot and the prophets reckoned that his day would soon be over. Strangely enough, the sector calmed down surprisingly fast.

In action Draget was calm and merciless, he knew how to manœuvre his men and enabled the Bande Noire to hit hard without getting touched. He won the respect of his men by his patience, which outmatched that of the Annamites, he would wait days observing a suspected region and struck only when he knew the moment to be right. If a native was suspected of liaison with the Viet he waited until he got the man redhanded and liquidated him on the spot—unlike Blairot, who woke up half a province to arrest a man and usually managed to shoot up an entire village before reaching a suspected cainha, by which time the suspect had taken to his heels. He refused to allow looting outside the official war zones, but when the Bande Noire got his authorisation they made more in one swoop than they had done before in a month of *razzia* and individual raiding parties.

But Draget, by the very integrity of his methods and the intransigence he showed towards abuse of them, earned himself the hostility of those who refused to play the game his way. The chief of his detractors was Captain Gobin, commanding F Company and the area of Buc Minh. He disliked Draget as a man, considering him a milksop; he was jealous because Draget in spite of his weedy appearance had not only come through the ranks but had done so with unabated brilliance; he cordially loathed Draget because he had spotted innumerable abuses in the Company's treatment of prisoners and suspects and he hated his guts for having warned the Company on several occasion of the known presence of Viets or of planned Viet activity—

each time the Captain had discarded the warning as useless and on each occasion it had proved to be the contrary and he had received a rap over the knuckles from higher up, following an official report from Draget.

Not far from the village of Buc Minh lay a wild stretch of country covered by impenetrable scrub, bamboo thickets and treacherous marshes. In the heart of the wasteland, the Viets had installed a redoubt and rallying point for their regional troops and agents. In spite of three years of effort, the Company had been unable to dislodge them. To approach the Viet nest of Tan Phu the only practicable means was to follow one of several vaguely sketched tracks that led towards it and then petered out in the scrub and bog; after that it was necessary to hack a way through. The Viet had surrounded the area with thousands of bamboo traps and trip-mines and every offensive which had been undertaken had invariably petered out with heavy casualties owing to the traps and mines, without a shot having been fired or a Viet seen. Draget had heard a lot of talk about Tan Phu and decided to go into the matter.

After a lot of study and reflection he sent off three men of the Bande Noire. Their role was to pose as deserters and to get themselves admitted into Tan Phu and to try to find out the tracks employed by the Viets and a plan of the traps surrounding the tracks as well as a plan of the village and the underground tunnels and rooms which were said to abound there. From aerial photos taken of the area it was impossible to spot a village as such, and the only logical conclusion was that the whole village had been constructed underground.

The Bande Noire was assembled and Draget asked for three volunteers for a special mission which promised a fifty-fifty chance of safe return. Three came forward after a few moments hesitation and Draget took them off to his office.

There he explained what he wanted and gave them three weeks in which to come back. Then came the hardest part: he had to persuade them to accept a god-almighty beating-up—he had reasoned that deserters as such would never be accepted as *bona fide* by the Viet who knew all the members of the Bande Noire; a European would not stand a chance as the Viet would ship the man off to another district. If, however, the three of them appeared on the outskirts of Tan Phu battered, bruised and bloody, with a tale of woe and injustice for some minor misdeed, thirsting to get a chance to revenge themselves, they stood a chance of getting into Tan Phu. Draget even went so far as to outline a plan to attack one or two of the road watch-towers which they could offer to lead, knowing the weak points of defence, and then slip away during the ensuing confusion. The important thing was that one at least managed to get back with a sufficiently clear plan of a safe approach to Tan Phu.

The men agreed, though the idea of getting beaten up didn't please them much. To make them feel happier Draget persuaded them that it would raise them enormously in the esteem of their fellows and the Europeans when the whole thing became known —meanwhile they were to pretend to have been punished for theft. The rest of the Bande Noire were warned that the men were going to be beaten up for a specific and temporarily secret reason, and that in the morning they would be posted as deserters; the only ones to know that they were not would be the Bande Noire and Draget.

The beating-up went off as planned and that night the three disappeared with their armament. The news spread around that three of the Bande Noire had deserted after they had been found stealing money in Draget's quarters and it caused a small stir for a day or two. There were even patrols sent out for them when Draget had reported their desertion; however, they had disappeared without leaving any trace and the matter was soon forgotten except by Draget's enemies, who pointed out that he was so useless that even his Bande Noire preferred to rejoin the Viet rather than stay under his orders and that he was just trying to cover up when he said that he had found them stealing money from his room.

Draget was delighted; the whole affair had started far better than he had hoped and with any luck the Viets would accept the three as *bona fide* renegades and let them have a crack at attacking a post or tower before the three-week limit was up. The most vociferous and vituperative of his critics was Captain Gobin at Buc Minh, who told all and sundry that he had always known Draget would be incapable of keeping the Bande Noire in hand. Draget had a quiet chuckle when this was reported to him and he thought how mad Gobin would be if only he knew how he was helping the Draget scheme.

Ten days later one of the three came back: it was late at night and he crept into the post without being noticed. He went straight to Draget's room and woke him up to give him the report. The three of them had left the Post and headed for Tan Phu. On the way they had decided to modify the plan. Only one of them would try to join the Viet, the other two would go on down to Saigon and lie low—they reckoned that three would have too much difficulty in getting away without arousing suspicion. They had drawn lots and he had been the winner. He had holed up in the brush the first day and in the evening had reached the scrub country round Tan Phu; once there, he found a track he had heard of and lay down to wait.

Finally a patrol had come by and from the voices of the men he had judged them to be Viets. He called to them for help. They had scattered, then cautiously surrounded him, suspicious in case of a trap: when they saw the state he was in and heard a résumé of his story they agreed to take him with them and he had found himself in Tan Phu. Once there, he was questioned and cross-questioned, then his wounds were dressed and he was left alone for a couple of days, though kept under observation. At the end of the third day he was called into the Viet commander and told that this story had been checked on and that he was expected to join and serve with the local Viet troops. He accepted eagerly and offered to lead a combat group against three towers whose weak points he knew. The offer was accepted, but he was warned that at first he would have to lead the way and go without arms to prove his sincerity.

On the fifth night he led a group out and they attacked a tower two kilometres from Buc Minh: the tower had been partially destroyed and the garrison had bolted. The seventh night he led another group out and they had blown up a small bridge under the noses of the sleeping sentinels. That night, the tenth night, he had led a group for the third time, they had attacked another tower near Buc Minh and he had fallen as though shot and rolled into a paddy-field. The others had seen him go down and judging the resistance of the post to be too fierce had called off the attack and disappeared into the night, leaving him for dead.

He then launched into a detailed description of the track leading into the stronghold of Tan Phu which he had passed six times. Each time he had noted the different traps, over which the Viets laid runners of bamboo in order to pass in safety. He had memorised them and drew a rough sketch of the track and also of the underground system with the main openings he had managed to spot; the latter were all camouflaged and some of them were in the banks and dikes of the surrounding marshland and had to be found by diving under the water—they were constructed on a siphon system. He was sure that he could lead the way to the stronghold if they went by night and affirmed that there were important stocks of mines and munitions hidden in the underground chambers. He estimated the overall strength of the Viet to be two hundred, though it changed from day to day as a large number came and left nightly, the place being used as a relay station for units changing sectors.

Draget reacted fast. He got up, dressed, and went straight off to wake up the Battalion Commander. What he had to say was important enough to risk waking up the boss in the middle of the night and once he had heard Draget's plans he would forget to bawl him out. He went up to the Major's room and woke him. Before he had had time to wake up thoroughly, Draget was already launched into his story. He explained how he had tricked up the stealing of his money and the desertion of the Bande Noire men and reported the desertion so that it would be officially recorded and patrols would be sent out after them. It had been the only way in which to guarantee that the Viet check-up on the deserters' story would be satisfactory. Then he outlined his plan. He would take in the Bande Noire the following night, led by the man who had come back. They would get into the stronghold, place themselves at the main underground entrances and get to work with dynamite—at the same time Captain Gobin from Buc Ninh would send out three platoons to create a diversion on the outskirts as though they were trying to find a path in, making as much noise as possible.

When the platoons heard the first sticks of dynamite go off they were to be led in by his scout and help to mop up. No one was to be told until two hours before the diversion was due—that way there could be no possible security leak. The Major accepted the outlines of the plan and they worked till dawn to straighten out the kinks.

The plan started just before sundown. An armoured car patrol was coming back from a routine run, the two cars were on a secondary road which skirted the scrub country round Tan Phu; when they were about abreast of the stronghold one of them skidded off the road and bogged down in the bordering paddy-field. After a half-hour struggle to get it out, the second car gave up and radioed through to Buc Minh for a platoon to come out to guard the car till the morning. Against his will Captain Gobin was obliged to send a platoon along—armoured cars were valuable and he couldn't risk having one taken or wrecked in his area. At the same time thirty men of the Bande Noire, heavily armed and carrrying several short bamboo ladders, dynamite and detonators, were splitting up into small groups and closing in on their point of rendezvous, a watch-tower four miles from Tan Phu. They drifted in over the space of two hours on different trucks which were Saigon-bound.

The garrison of the tower was known to be extremely hostile

to the Viet and there was no danger of a leak. The truck-drivers were all Saigon-bound and noticed nothing very odd—they were used to giving lifts to small parties of what they took to be watch-tower auxiliaries.

Draget joined them just before dusk and they settled down to go over the actions of each man until everyone was thoroughly briefed in his particular role. Their kick-off time was to be just after midnight. At midnight an enormous breakdown truck, escorted by another platoon from Buc Minh, made its way along to the stranded armoured car—Captain Gobin was furious but could not refuse the second platoon, breakdown trucks were even more costly than armoured cars—it was just one of those days.

By three o'clock the Bande Noire had reached the track that led into Tan Phu. Slowly and silently they crept along it, taking the greatest possible care to make no noise—after two hours they were clear of the track and the man who had come back from there placed the men at the entrances to the underground—there was still half an hour to go before dawn.

At three o'clock the Battalion Commander arrived at Buc Minh, woke up Captain Gobin and told him what was going on. After a rapid survey of the situation he told him to get another section ready within fifteen minutes and to take it along to where the armoured car was broken down. Once there, he was to take three platoons and start beating through the scrub in the direction of the track that led into Tan Phu—he was to reach the track by five-thirty when the dawn broke. There would be a guide waiting to lead him through to the stronghold—once joined up with the Bande Noire he was to assure the complete destruction of the place.

Captain Gobin was livid that Draget had pulled off the idea and had succeeded in getting into the place he had tried to approach in vain for over two years, but was fully resolved to cash in on the situation once there. By five-thirty he was in place with his three platoons and waiting impatiently for the guide. As the latter appeared there came a series of explosions and bursts of fire from Tan Phu. Draget and the Bande Noire had touched off the first sticks of dynamite, intended to block the Viet in their tunnels, and were shooting down those on the surface. The guide led them off down the track, insisting that the platoons follow in single file—that was too slow for the Captain, however, who had the men advance in three columns; before they had reached Tan Phu the platoons had already lost fifteen men wounded in the traps, another twenty had to stay behind to protect them. Captain Gobin arrived finally on the scene with only half the expected strength to find Draget and his Bande Noire busily dynamiting tunnels and shooting down stray Viets whenever they popped up out of the ground and tried to make a break for it.

Draget gave him a rapid survey of the situation and the Captain said that he had already been briefed by the Battalion Commander and would take over. Draget agreed politely and asked in a casual way if the rest of his Company was on the way—he had been expecting to see three platoons arrive and there only seemed to be one and a half.

The Captain replied curtly that the guide had led them into some traps and that his men had fallen into them. Surprised, Draget said nothing and waited. The Captain said that he had no further need for the Bande Noire and that Draget could leave. The latter called his men together and after handing over the rest of the dynamite they started back. As they went they heard the explosions continue amidst almost unceasing gunfire.

For a moment Draget nearly turned and went back, thinking that perhaps the Viet had found a means of counter-attacking, then decided it was better not to. On the way back down the track they passed, from time to time, small groups of men carrying wounded and noticed that they were all to one side or other of the track. Draget called the man who had been to Tan Phu and asked him how it was the men had not followed the track or had he mistaken the way and taken them up an unknown path. The man answered somewhat sullenly that the Captain had ordered the men to advance in three columns instead of

Draget's men boarded the truck

single file and had brushed aside his protestations, saying that he was little better than a Viet anyway and that the Bande Noire had nothing to teach him. Draget smiled.

They got back to the road and found a truck there, one of several waiting to bring back the men and eventual captured material and prisoners. Draget pushed his men aboard and they made their way back to HQ. Once there, Draget led his men to their quarters and once they had stripped off their gear gathered them together; he thanked them for the night's work and the co-operation they had shown during the first part of the plan and then calling them round him they tried to estimate the exact amount of damage they had caused. They finally settled on a figure of some thirty Viet killed on the surface and at least twenty tunnels blocked, before the arrival of the Captain. Draget himself had been responsible for at least six Viet.

As he was preparing to go and report to the Major, one of the Bande Noire NCOs came up to him and apologised for the way they had all felt about him up till then. They had thought that he was afraid of the Viet, now they knew that he was a man a real officer and one of them. He could wait to jump but when he did he killed swiftly like a tiger and yet he was gentle once the killing was over. From that day the Bande Noire always referred to Draget as 'the gentle tiger'.

The final result of Draget's plan was the complete destruction of Tan Phu. The cost: sixteen wounded from the Captain's Company—fifteen from traps and one from dynamite. The reward —a Croix de Guerre apiece for the wounded. A slightly higher Croix de Guerre for the Captain and a Croix de Guerre with Palm for Draget and a proposition to move up in rank in the order of the Legion of Honour. All of which settled nothing in the relations of Draget and the Captain, who was trebly disgusted by the fact that the Bande Noire had had no wounded, that Draget had succeeded where he had always failed, that Draget had received higher official awards. To soothe his feelings once he had heard of the 'gentle tiger', he took to calling Draget the 'gelded tom-cat'.

Chapter

13

IT TOOK A few months for the Battalion to settle down to the new order of things and in the interim the men, denied the outlet of indiscriminate Viet-hunting and looting, turned to the local bars and cafés to let off steam. The results were often wild and woolly and it took quite a while for everybody to forget the good old days.

One of the Companies the hardest hit by the change was C Company and with it Captain Blanche who had become, in a very short time, an ardent disciple of Colonel Angeli. The Company had the reputation of being the hardest hitting and most decorated of the Battalion and the reputation had been well earned. The sergeant who ran the company's information service openly claimed to having bumped off three hundred odd Viet in four years; about three-quarters of them were prisoners of no value. There were several others hard at work to catch up on his record. Naturally enough when the new régime came into full swing they all felt a little bit lost, and to counter-attack the boredom of their increasingly pacific occupations the bottles began to take a beating.

About a month after the change-over I managed to get another Sunday off and, as usual, dropped down to see Hartz. The mess was in full swing when I arrived at Cau Chi, even though it was only ten in the morning. They were having a celebration to fête the arrival of an NCO who had just come back from Sidi Bel Abbes for a second period. Even the locally married had abandoned their wives for the day and, in spite of the heat, the drinks kept on flowing all day. I had to get back to HQ that night and took the opportunity of a lift with an armoured patrol car that was going back to Loc Ninh at five in the afternoon. Patrols of two to three armoured cars opened the road each morning and closed it to circulation each evening. They were frequently used for cadging lifts between posts. When I left the mess the party was still going full blast and the men's canteen and the village bars were not leaving the mess far behind. The ride back to HQ, perched on the engine cowling of the armoured car, sobered me up considerably, which was just as well. On getting back to Loc Ninh I found that I had to replace the NCO in charge of the night guard; he had gone sick with a bout of malaria.

Being sergeant of the guard at night was no joke—each round was nearly a mile and I had to keep on the go in order to prevent the sentinels from falling asleep, and there were fifteen of them. Sunday nights it was plain murder as most of the men had been out in the village all day on the razzle. But we had an unwritten law for Sunday nights: we never turned in a man for sleeping at his post, it would have meant a court-martial for the culprit; we just slapped him around till he came to and sobered up.

What with one thing and another I was dead beat when midnight came and I was ready to massacre the next snoring sentry I found. I had just got back to the guardroom when the telephone rang. It was the night radio shift calling to warn me that C Company had sent a crash call for help. The Viet had blown up one of their buildings and were attacking in force. Knowing that I as B.S.M. was on duty they had rung me so that I could go and warn the Battalion Commander; none of the radio gang felt courageous enough to tell him.

I first woke the stand-by duty NCO to take over and then went along to see the Commanding Officer with the message from C Company. I think he must have had quite a Sunday too. When he got the gist of the message he threw a fit of temperament and then told me to roust out the intervention patrol, an armoured car patrol, warn Captain Baudoin and to go along myself and to radio back as soon as I had arrived to detail any developments.

Within ten minutes we were on our way, though the platoon was short of ten or twelve men who must have been sleeping in town on the quiet. We were only a couple of miles from Cau Chi when the leading patrol car went up on a mine. Two of the crew were killed and the other two wounded. We picked up the wounded, left a group behind to guard the wreckage and hurried on, spraying the surrounding countryside with bursts of everything we had as we went.

We got to the post to find everything relatively calm, though there were occasional bursts of automatic weapon fire coming from the outskirts of the village. Inside the post a couple of buildings were in ruins and another on fire; the confusion seemed to have been pretty general.

I found Captain Blanche, bloodstained, black-faced and in rags, and told him that the CO had asked for an immediate message with essential details. He said that he hadn't the time but gave me the details and asked me to pass them through. I went off to the radio cabin and sent through what he had given me. 'Platoon building mined at eleven thirty; two men killed outright, rest of platoon on guard duty, kitchen storeroom destroyed and burnt, Captain's bungalow destroyed and burnt, armoured car lost on the way.' I was finishing the message when Captain Blanche came in and told me to add that another armoured car, from his local patrol, had just radioed in that it had a front wheel blown off by a mine. The armoured group had gone to the aid of a small post held by auxiliaries that was being heavily attacked by the Viets and had run into the mine on the way back. He would have to send off a platoon in protection and wanted to know if he could use the Intervention Platoon from HQ. In case of a renewed

Viet attack on C Company he preferred to keep his own men in the post. The O.K. came through within five minutes. The Intervention Platoon took off straight away. I stayed behind to wait while Captain Blanche drew up a rough report of the night attack which he wanted me to take back with me, so that he wouldn't have to go down to HQ in person.

Hartz, who was the Company Sergeant-Major, joined us and the two of us sat down in the mess while the Captain worked out a rough draft. Hartz and I went over to the bar and had a beer and as we drank it he told me a little of what had happened. Most of the NCOs and quite a few of the men were sleeping out in the village as usual. Round eleven-thirty he had been woken by the sound of someone trying to get into his cainha. His congaie, also awake, called out to ask who it was. The answer was in Annamite. His congaie grabbed him, whispered that it was the Viet and that they were asking if he were there. Hartz jumped out of bed, grabbed up his clothes and slid out by the back door while the woman let the Viet in by the front. As he got out into the street there had been a series of explosions, the buildings in the post going up, followed by bursts of automatic weapon fire coming from all directions. He had been so scared that he didn't wait to dress. He ran the hundred yards to the post naked and barefoot in ten seconds flat, dodging odd bursts of fire as he went. Once inside the post he whipped into his shorts, dashed over to the mortar emplacement and started to belt mortar shells into the surrounding countryside. By then most of the men had got back to the post, the sleepers had come to and were at their action stations and, after an hour of heavy and continuous firing, the Viet had decided that the opposition was too strong and had melted away into the night.

When things had quietened off a bit they had scouted around the post and had come across a long length of telephone wire which ran from the wrecked buildings to the outer defences of the village. The Viet had managed to creep up to the walls of the buildings, slip in some plastic charges linked to the wire, then fired the charges before they had properly surrounded the post, otherwise it would surely have been a goner. The platoon that had been on guard was in luck—had the men been in their building the whole platoon would have been killed. As it was, the two killed had been excused guard duty since they were down with dysentery.

Hartz was just going to give me a lot of other details, when the Captain called me over and gave me his report. There was still an armoured car waiting outside the post; it was the one from HQ which hadn't blown up and, since everything seemed to have quietened down, he told me to get back to HQ with it straight away. There was still an hour before dawn and the drive back to HQ perched on the cowling was far from being the joy-ride of the previous evening. Every bush seemed to hide a Viet and I must have seen the entire Viet army by the time we got back to Loc Ninh.

I went straight to the Battalion Commander's quarters, woke him, handed him Captain Blanche's report and, when he asked if things really quietened down, assured him that it wasn't worth his while to get up. That finished with, I went on back to the guardroom to see if my relief wanted me to take over again. Luckily he didn't and I was able to get off to bed. It was only five and I hoped to get in a couple of hours' sleep—I needed them.

I had barely had the time to lie down when an off-duty sentry came in and told me that Lieutenant Draget wanted to see me urgently. Utterly weary and in a filthy temper, I struggled back into my clothes and went over to his office, trying to imagine what the devil he could want. He was sitting behind his desk as pale as a ghost, nervous and fidgety. When I came in he told me to shut the door and to sit down. I sat and waited, by then really worried, and hurriedly rattled through my mind all the possible misdeeds I could have committed in the last twenty-four hours, or even before—but I just couldn't find one to fit in with a five-o'clock-in-the-morning summons from a security officer. At last he broke the silence and asked me if I had been sergeant of the guard that night. Even while I was answering yes, I had an appalling feeling that I knew what was up. Some stupid bastard had deserted and he had just been warned. There was always hell to pay for the NCO on duty when a man deserted. He was automatically responsible and usually broken for not having had the initiative to foresee the deserter's intentions— it was rather primitive justice, but in the Foreign Legion stripes flew away with the greatest of ease.

Draget's next questions however, knocked the deserter idea on the head, which was a pity as I couldn't dig up another theory to fit and felt even more lost. He wanted to know all my movements since I had taken over the guard the evening before. How I had been dressed and who I had seen. It just didn't make any sense. I told him that I had been away since midnight, that I had been at Cau Chi in the C Company post and that I had just come back with a report for the Battalion Commander. Not content with that, he wanted to know how many men of the Intervention Platoon had gone along and how they were dressed. I neither knew nor remembered, which seemed to upset him.

Finally, after more than half an hour of beating around the bush, he came out with it. He had been woken up by Blanchet, the Police Commissioner, who, in turn, had been woken up by a native. The native had arrived at the police station with a tale of murder and robbery. He lived on the outskirts of the village and his next-door neighbours, three of them, had been beaten, robbed and then shot by six Europeans dressed in black, and who apparently had then taken the direction of our post. The native, having heard the racket next-door, had slipped out into his garden and hidden behind a tree from which he had seen the men. Once they had gone he had entered the neighbours' house and when he had seen the bodies had gone straight round to Blanchet.

Normally six armed men couldn't leave or enter the post without the knowledge of the sergeant of the guard and, as a result, I was suspected of having been in connivance with them—if they really were Europeans, Légionnaires, and came from the post. The affair had taken place about two o'clock. Blanchet had gone off with a group of policemen to check and, until he came back and until Draget was sure I had been to Cau Chi and had not left there till after two, he was going to consider me as suspect. I told him that he could check on my departure and arrival with the armoured car group. He telephoned, got a satisfactory reply and I was in the clear. He made me promise not to say a word to anybody and let me go back to bed.

For the next three days the HQ post was a hotbed of rumours. Everyone knew that something was up, but only a handful of us and, presumably, the six men involved, knew what had happened. Finally one of the six went off to the Police Commissioner and told him what had happened, who had gone with him and asked for his spontaneous confession to be taken into into consideration. We shipped the six of them to the Saigon military prison the next day. The damn fools had wanted to play at being little heroes and had set off to try to ambush the Viet. On the way they decided to stop in a cainha which was showing a light. They thought there might be a Viet in it. Once in the cainha they had found an old man and two women who were naturally petrified at the sight of the armed men. One of the women had tried to bolt; they had knocked her down and shot her. Panic-stricken by what they had done they decided to kill the other two, take their odd bits of jewellery and the little cash they could find, and trust to luck that the incident would be put down to the score of the Viet or the Caodai. They had reckoned without the neighbour.

It was an unfortunate incident and did a lot to upset the new Battalion Commander's efforts to instil confidence in French justice in the local population. From our point of view it was no joke either, there was an inevitable tightening up of interior discipline and the night guard became a nightmare. The six of them had used a hole in the barbed-wire defences to go in and

out and it turned out that the hole had been the main thorough-
fare for men with girls in town for months past.

Meantime at Cau Chi they had had an incredible stroke of
luck. The day after the night attack there had been a traffic jam
in the village, caused by an overturned truck. One of the villagers
had noticed in a taxi the Viet commander of the Battalion which
had tried to take the post. He had used the villager's house as a
command post. The villager was one of the rare natives who
was completely pro-French and two of his daughters were
married to men in the Company. He hurried along to Captain
Blanche and reported what he had seen. As discreetly as possible,
armed only with revolvers hidden in their pockets, a group of
men surrounded the taxi, and at a given signal, wrenched open
the doors and dragged out the occupants. They were five,
including the chauffeur, all in ordinary native dress, and turned
out to be the Commander of the Viet Battalion with his staff on
their way to Saigon to report to their superiors. (The Viet had a
regional HQ somewhere in Saigon.)

Since they were not in uniform Captain Blanche had no scruples.
They were treated as ordinary suspects and none too gently at
that. They were fed just enough to keep them alive and spent the
days rebuilding what they had blown up. Their refreshment
consisted of blows from rifle-butts and sticks. At dusk they were
'questioned' for an hour or two. The only thing they would
admit to was having attacked the post and after five days they all
died 'trying to escape', having just admitted that they were
members of the battalion which had attacked the post. It was
only then that Lieutenant Draget got the news and he was mad
with rage. It was just what he was trying to stop. He and Captain
Blanche, however, were at daggers drawn and it was only one
of a series of pinpricks which the Captain used to goad
Lieutenant Draget.

Chapter
14

By june, a couple of months after the departure of Colonel Angeli and the others, we still hadn't received the reinforcements we hoped for and the manpower situation in the battalion was becoming serious. Apart from the men lost in action, the wounded and the sick, there had been a marked increase in crime and disciplinary infractions which meant that the men involved were shipped off to prison or the Legion's Indochinese disciplinary centre.

The new troops arriving from Africa were all vitally needed for the Regiment's two battalions in Tonkin, and to supplement four other regiments of Foreign Legion infantry and parachutists who had been suffering heavy and consistent losses. The rare driblets effected to our battalion were those too old or too untried to be of any use for the heavy fighting up North, and barely covered our overall losses. Our officer situation was equally critical. At HQ we were reduced to four officers and the Companies to an officer per company. The net results was an appallingly heavy increase in the responsibilities of the NCOs and a general decrease in discipline and morale of the men.

From where I sat behind my desk I was in a good position to appreciate what was going on. I was snowed under with dossiers, reports and punishments, concerning the different companies, and soon had no time for anything at all but paper work. I was even obliged to give up going out on night patrols, which up till then had formed my main source of exercise and relaxation. The only bright spot was the fact the Battalion Commander, who had no second-in-command, left more and more of the work in my hands which meant that the Company Sergeant-Majors and I had far more liberty to fix things up between ourselves, before certain matters went too high—if we felt that the man involved was getting a rough deal.

The Legion forming part of the French Army, all our paper work was based on the French Army system. Apart from the multiple copies needed for everything the formulae were absolute and the slightest departure from a given formula meant the re-establishment of any given dossier. It was thanks to the red tape and iron-clad traditions in force that Hartz, of C Company, and I managed to save Lance-Sergeant Marais from being reduced to the ranks.

Marais, through no fault of his own, had the kind of bad luck which occasionally befell commanders of small isolated posts. He had been put in charge of the small blockhouse which guarded the bridge across the Cau Coi, a few miles down the main Saigon road from Cau Chi. Captain Blanche had chosen him because he wasn't of much use in a platoon and because his age and dimming wits made him too slow in action. It was an ideal job, however, the pick of all the jobs in the sector, and had always gone to men of Marais' stamp. Men who were no longer of any use on patrol or in action yet had accumulated enough years of service to be trusted. A nice quiet little job where age, medalled bosom and suitably low rank drew the eye of passing brass-hats who would occasionally stop for an old-soldierly chat. They got all the right answers and went away feeling good, feeling they had had a heart-to-heart chat with the backbone of the old army, with an old-time scrapper in whose judgment an officer could have confidence. And Marais was all that. He kept the post at the bridge of Cau

An isolated post

Coi impeccable. By dint of swearing and bullying he had finally knocked into the heads of the seven dim-wits who composed his garrison that life would only be easy on condition that the place was kept clean, that they themselves kept clean, and that they realised he was the boss.

The post itself was down below the bridge, on the river bank. Solidly built of logs with double earth-packed walls, it was a square, squat utilitarian building topped off with a tiled-roof watch-tower, from which the sentinel had a commanding view over the flat, bare expanse of marshes spreading away on all sides until they finally met the horizon. A triple tangle of barbed-wire defences running round the post through the river and round the bridge, which was closed at both ends at dusk with heavy barbed wire *chevaux de frise*, theoretically guaranteed protection against any hostile attack or sabotage of the bridge. Marais had had his men dredge out the part of the river bed in front of the post, which gave them a swimming pool, and periodically he made them cut and burn the vegetation growing in the defences so that the place always looked well kept. A fact which had earned him repeated felicitations from the Colonel of the Regiment—on his way to or from Saigon—and repeated hangovers from the drinks he took to celebrate each felicitation.

But for all that Marais was a serious man. Twice a week he had to go to Cau Chi to fetch stores and report to Captain Blanche. On the day in question, before setting out for the village, he called in Private Kryz, his second-in-command, and went through the usual routine of making him repeat the standing orders for the garrison of the bridge. The most important of these were, that no vehicle was to station on or near the bridge, that no unauthorised person was to be allowed to circulate in the marshes in the vicinity of the bridge unless expressly permitted to do so by the NCO in command of the post acting in accordance with the Commander of C Company. Kryz duly and mulishly repeated the roundelay and Marais left for the village at peace with the world, knowing that he had done everything according to regulations. As usual he left with the armoured car, which ran from Cau Chi to the bridge of Cau Coi every morning to open the road.

As soon as he got to Cau Chi, Marais went along to report to Captain Blanche, picked up the mail for his men, saw about his stores and, after a beer in the mess, went into the village to buy a few odds and ends. He never stayed long, however, and within half an hour he was ready to start back. The Company always ran him back to the bridge in the truck that went down to Saigon for the Company stores; by eight o'clock they had left Cau Chi.

They had no sooner got within sight of the bridge than Marais realised something must have gone wrong. His seven men were clustered around what looked like bodies on the ground and there was a command car parked by the bridge, which was strictly against orders. As the truck drew up behind the car the men turned and Kryz came towards Marais, with a face as white as a sheet, to announce that since he had left two colonels had been killed and one seriously wounded. While his men unloaded the stores from the truck Marais got the story out of Kryz.

Shortly after seven, about five minutes after Marais had left for the village, a command car had pulled up alongside the blockhouse and three men got out. They all had shot-guns and game bags. Kryz had gone up to them and told them that it was forbidden to park there or to go into the marshes. One of the three had pooh-poohed and announced that they were three colonels from Saigon, that they had the authorisation of the Colonel of the Regiment and that they wanted two men to go along with them as beaters.

Kryz hadn't known what to do. He spoke very little French, understood less and was terrified of colonels. After a short hesitation he had told Lopez and Schulz to get their rifles and to go along with the colonels. The one who had done all the speaking had repeated that all was in order and that Kryz had nothing to worry about. He said that he knew from Saigon that there were no Viet in the neighbourhood and that there were plenty of duck in the marshes and hinted that they would leave a little something so that the men could buy a drink later in the day.

Schulz, Lopez and the three colonels had gone off into the marshes and five minutes later there had been a burst of firing, shouts and then silence. Kryz hadn't dared go off to see what was up. Even if there had been an ambush he only had four men left and he couldn't leave the bridge unguarded. Schulz and Lopez had finally come into sight carrying a man between them. It was the one who had been wounded. They had sent three men back to pick up the two dead. He couldn't give any further details, so Marais called over Schulz.

Schulz and Lopez had been sent off into the marshes to make a semicircular sweep. The colonels had told them to make as much noise as possible to scare the ducks. They had only just started off when they heard several shots in quick succession followed by a shout for help. They both turned and started back for the dike as fast as they could go—shouts and shots could only mean one thing out there. As they neared the dike they slowed down and advanced more cautiously, caught sight of the dike and saw the three hunters sprawled over it—two were obviously dead and the third was thrashing around in agony. Not wanting to receive the same treatment, they approached with the greatest caution and spotted a bunch of armed natives racing off down the dike. They opened up and fired a magazine apiece, without any apparent effect, then reached the dike and made for the wounded man. He seemed to have most of his chest blown away, so they ripped off his shirt and jacket and did what they could with their emergency dressings. He was still sufficiently conscious to burble out that a gang of armed natives had appeared from nowhere, shot them down and disappeared with their guns. He begged them to hurry him back to the post, then fainted.

Schulz and Lopez had agreed to get out of there fast; they slung their rifles and, grabbing the wounded man by his shoulders and legs, started off back towards the bridge. They didn't dare leave him and go back for help in case there would be another ambush waiting for the return. Slowly and painfully they struggled back towards the bridge, weighed down by their burden—the bridge wasn't far but the dike had not been built for that kind of traffic and they were constantly slipping and sliding into the marsh on either side. It had taken them a good ten minutes to make it back to the post and when they got there they were completely foundered and unable to do a thing for at least a quarter of an hour.

After hearing what Kryz and Schulz had to say, Marais went over to have a look at the victims. The colonel who had been wounded was coming to, so he decided to ask him if he wanted to go down to Saigon on the truck or wait till an ambulance could be procured. He managed to tell Marais that he was a surgeon in Saigon and asked him to get him to a hospital as fast as he could; he added that they had left their papers in the car and that the key was in his pocket.

His men having finished unloading the stores, Marais got them to lift in the dead and wounded while he went off to the command car and got their identity papers. He gave the latter to Kryz and told him to go with the truck. Barely ten minutes had gone by since Marais had arrived from Cau Chi and it wasn't till he saw the truck start off towards Saigon that the full horror of the situation struck him.

By chance the Viet hadn't cut the telephone line, which linked him with Cau Chi; they cut it most nights as telephone wire came in very handy for their remote control mines. He got Captain Blanche on the line and told him what had happened and what he had done. The Captain told him not to worry and said he would be over straight away. A few minutes later the captain arrived. He questioned Marais, Schulz and Lopez, told them not to worry, that the fault was entirely on the colonels' side, and left to report the news to the Battalion Commander.

But it really was Marais' unlucky day. Just before midday the Colonel's car drew up coming from Saigon. The Colonel got out in a blind rage and blew the hell out of Marais. He had heard the news in Saigon, by chance. He would, he said, have Marais busted—he wasn't fit to wear stripes, let alone command a post. He was going to have him replaced immediately and as for the two idiots who had escorted the colonels in the marshes they were good for sixty days apiece. Marais tried to say that he hadn't been there but soon gave up and let the Colonel rant on. After a five-minute tirade the Colonel went on his way. He stopped in at Cau Chi and repeated the performance for Captain Blanche's benefit and then left for Battalion HQ. There he gave us the same treatment, and by that time black with rage, took off for Regimental HQ. He had the finest command of vitriolic army French that I ever heard.

The next morning we received an official confirmation of his outburst and orders to establish the necessary papers and reports.

for Marais' degradation and the sixty days apiece for Lopez and Schulz. Hartz and Captain Blanche had come down to the Battalion HQ to find out what the Colonel had had to say and, after I had told them and shown them the confirmation, Captain Blanche went off to see the Battalion Commander. He came back with a long face and said there was nothing to be done. We would just have to go ahead and carry out the order.

The stupid part about the whole affair lay in the fact that not only was Marais guilty of nothing at all but also that nobody except the Colonel wanted to see him either degraded or moved from his post. At Cau Chi he was the right man in the right job. If anyone had to get punished it should logically have been Kryz, whom Marais had left in charge during his absence. Hartz and I were fond of Marais and we decided that, Colonel or no Colonel, we would do our best to help him and Lopez and Schulz at the same time.

By devious means we managed to keep their dossiers travelling around for nearly three months. They kept coming back for completion, for inclusion of this and that, for signatures and supplementary details, until finally the Colonel lost patience with the whole affair and let it drop. Though his orders to let the matter drop were accompanied by a scathing letter about the inability of the Battalion to establish the simplest documents correctly and an open threat of punishment for those responsible the next time such a thing should occur.

Apart from the Marais affair, we were going through a very bad period in the Battalion and I had become heartily sick of the never-ending stream of rape, desertion and general indiscipline which meant, to me, an incredible amount of the most tedious kind of routine paper-work. It was, therefore, with considerable joy that I welcomed the arrival of my successor in August— a dyed-in-the-wool bureaucrat, fifteen years in the Legion, and fourteen of them in offices. Within a couple of weeks I had passed him over the work in hand and applied for my immediate transfer.

The CO granted my request and agreed to my transfer to C Company. A double joy for me as I was to be promoted to Sergeant the same day. Afterwards I often wondered how I managed to come through my six months in charge of the HQ office without being reduced to the ranks or thrown into prison for gross insubordination and general incompetence.

Chapter
15

BEFORE I WAS due to join C Company orders suddenly came through from the Regimental CO that the Company was to move from Cau Chi. It was to be replaced by a company of the Baodai regulars. The Bao Dai régime or Vietnam had by September 1952 succeeded in putting on war footing a small regular army, units of which were used in pacified zones or holding troops. C Company was to take over an area in the Sector of Tay Ninh, some fifty miles further on and nearly on the Cambodian frontier. But, and it was a large but, C Company would have to build its own post. The area allocated had been in Viet hands for years and it was to be brought back under French control.

When the news came through, Captain Blanche decided to go up to his new area and have a look around before moving in. He took Hartz with him and on the way dropped in at HQ and asked if I would care to go along as well. As soon as we got to Tay Ninh he went to see the Commander of the sector, who was the Colonel of the North African Cavalry Regiment our battalion had replaced at Loc Ninh on New Year's Eve. He came out a few minutes later looking very glum and told us that the post we were to build was about fifteen miles from Tay Ninh in the middle of a forest. The road leading to it was only safe for

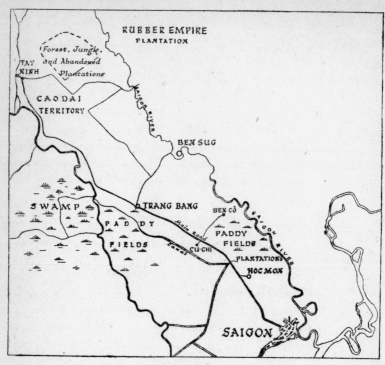

The new forest sector

half the distance and we would have to have an armoured car escort for the rest of the way. To top off the bad news he added that the watch-towers along the road and the nearest post were manned by Caodai.

It took us half an hour to reach the site, a clearing in the middle of the forest which lay in the centre of a dip in the ground through which ran a stream. From what the Captain told us Hartz and I gathered that the Company would have to build a post there and once it was built push on further down the road towards the Saigon River, which was five miles away. There the company would have to throw a bridge across the river, build another post, rebuild the twenty miles of road between Tay Ninh and the river and clear the jungle and brush from round the posts and on either side of the road. It sounded like an awful lot of work for one company, especially right in the middle of hostile country. The idea behind the whole plan was to get the road opened and safe for circulation so as to facilitate the reopening of a number of large rubber plantations which had been abandoned for years. The most unpleasant part of it was that we would be one company alone against the Viet who were particularly strong in that area. They had their regional headquarters somewhere in the offing and must have kept at least three battalions there in permanence as well as training camps, rest centres and depots of ammunitions and stores.

I felt a lot less cheerful about my transfer when I got back to Loc Ninh and the comparative comfort of the Battalion HQ for which I developed a sudden affection.

Two days after our visit to the site, C Company passed through Loc Ninh, en route for their new emplacement. A convoy of thirty trucks piled high with the inevitable stores, belongings and bric-à-brac of a company on the move. For once, however, there was not a single congaie to be seen. They had all been left behind at Cau Chi and we could spot the married men on the trucks by the glumness of their expressions. I still had fifteen days to go before I joined them, thanks to which I missed the ambush the Viet had prepared for the Company on the road leading to the new site. Two trucks were blown up and half a dozen men wounded, but apart from that there was not too much damage done and the Viet did not push their advantage. It seemed to have been meant more as a warning of things to come than an effort to wipe the Company out on the spot.

The day before I was due to join C Company I took the day off to pack my gear and take leave of my friends in the village and the CCB. Inevitably it meant far too many drinks all round and it was late by the time I staggered to bed after the final round in the NCOs' mess. In the middle of the night I was awakened by the most appalling racket. Windows and doors were banging and crashing, a terrific wind was playing merry hell with the roofs and the trees and the rain that was coming down fell in a solid sheet. I tried to struggle out to see what was going on but it took me three attempts before I could get through my door and on to the terrace outside. At the first two attempts I had been blown back into my room. In the end I managed to get as far as the guardroom. There I found the NCO on duty tearing his hair out. Nothing worked any more. Within five minutes the wind had knocked out the electricity, the telephone, and had blown down trees all over the place. Every time he had tried to get somewhere inside the post to check up on his sentries he had found the way barred by telephone poles, branches or raging torrents. We had been caught by the tail end of a cyclone.

Tail end or not, it didn't stop blowing or raining until well into the morning and, when finally it eased up, we realised that the village was flooded. All the streams and rivers had burst their banks, all the roads were feet under water, most of the buildings in the post had been damaged either by the wind or by falling trees and we were all worn out, wet through and, for the first time in months or years, really cold. To top it all off, the radio aerials had been carried away and it was not till the afternoon that we managed to get into contact with the other posts and the outside world in general. Everywhere in the sector it had been the same and everywhere the roads were cut and the waters were rising.

As soon as dawn had begun to break we had formed rescue parties to save as many of the villagers and as much of their livestock as possible. In the village the loss of life was low, but in the surrounding countryside of low-lying rice-fields quite a few families had been surprised and swept away. The only bright spot for us was that we knew the Viet troops must have taken an even worse beating from the cyclone as the majority had to live in the open.

We lived in a state of splendid isolation for four days before the waters began to go down. Then it was a period of feverish activity to get the main road patched up in the places where it had been washed away. It was a full week before the first truck got through from Saigon and was able to continue as far as the Cambodian frontier. The secondary roads and tracks were out of commission for at least a fortnight, and even after that it was a tricky business driving along them. If a truck was too heavily loaded the roads just gave way and the truck squatted down on its axles till another came along to haul it out of trouble.

Naturally, little was done in the way of Viet-hunting during that period, and they must have had enough trouble of their own to look after, for they left us well alone.

Before leaving for C Company I had been called in by the Battalion Commander, who said goodbye, and before letting me go he added that he had told Captain Blanche that he wanted me to take over from Hartz who was shortly due to leave. He went on to say that I had better go round and see Lieutenant Dindon, the Battalion Treasurer, who was responsible for the finances of the companies. I went round to Lieutenant Dindon's office and told him that the CO had sent me to see him before I left for C Company. What he had to tell me gave me no pleasure whatsoever. The Company was in the hell of a mess financially; clothing and money and stores were missing. Hartz and Captain Blanche had tried to make good by declaring an enormous amount of material destroyed during the night attack at Cuchi, but even though their estimate had been accepted the Company was still in a hole. He warned me that if I took over from Hartz as Company Sergeant-Major I would have to verify everything with the greatest of care, especially so since the Company had by radio declared losses due to the cyclone which were absurdly heavy and would certainly be the object of an investigation by the Quartermaster General, who was expected to make a round of the companies within a few weeks. With that he wished me luck and said goodbye.

I didn't like any of it and suddenly wished I had never asked for a transfer. In the French Army each company was responsible for the feeding of its own men and drew the cash monthly, on top of which there was a fifteen-day security stock of dried goods which counted as a permanent credit. The company funds were held by the CO, who was meant to be responsible but frequently left all that to his CSM. Normally companies had a float from which were drawn funds for food and canteen expenses, but from what Dindon said C Company was damn nearly bankrupt. Once an incoming CSM had countersigned on taking over from his predecessor he was responsible for any errors from then on. I knew little enough about accountancy to hate the idea of it and saw my dreams of going into a combat platoon vanishing in thin air.

In the end I managed to get on my way. The C Company provision truck, which had got stuck in Saigon by the cyclone, arrived in Loc Ninh on October 4th, a week later. Apart from the stores there were six men from the Company who had gone down on a twenty-four hour pass to Cau Chi to see the wives they had left behind and who were coming back broke and battered after a week's leave, having been trapped by the cyclone. I had my gear put onto the truck and climbed up amongst the wrecks for what was to prove a nerve-wracking journey. The driver may have known the road well, but it was still under water for most of the way and he drove as though he were on a race track. Once we reached Tay Ninh and the branch road to Suo Hiep, however, he was obliged to slow down. The road, though comparatively dry, was too bad for speed in a loaded truck and we took the next fifteen miles at a slow lurching crawl under the escort of an armoured car.

In spite of the havoc reported by radio it was a surprise to see how the clearing had taken on the aspect of a post about to be built. In the two weeks prior to the flooding they had managed to get the main foundations laid and a tower and one building finished, on the outside at least. The platoons were under canvas and had placed themselves on the rising ground within the perimeter of barbed wire defences. The post itself was bang in the middle of the hollow, surrounded by water and only accessible by means of a series of greasy tree-trunks, laid end to end, which led from the dried ground to within the walls.

As soon as the truck stopped it was rapidly surrounded by a horde of hungry men who hadn't seen fresh stores or beer since the cyclone. I got off and went to present myself to Captain Blanche who was inside the post. I started across the log walk and, to everybody's delight, slipped off into the quagmire before I had got half-way. Fortunately it was not much more than knee-deep and I managed to get into the post without further mishap. The Captain had installed himself in a part of the one finished building and had it rigged up as a combined Company office, CO's office-bedroom-mess. The other half was the sick-bay.

I found Hartz and the Captain in the latter's part of the building and presented the clean half of myself as best I could. Blanche and Hartz were overjoyed that I had had my baptism so soon and made me feel better by saying that they went off the logs at least twice a day. Once the customary performance of presenting myself was through I left with Hartz to hunt up a dry spot where I could dump my gear and sleep. In the end, with the Captain's approval I took one of the two beds in the sick-bay. The sick-bay attendant slept in the other. The sick were all shipped off to the military hospital at Tay Ninh and the place was only used for dressings and treatments during the day. It suited me fine so I sent a couple of prisoners off to get my gear and, once it had arrived, arranged things as much as possible—inside the post the floors were ankle-deep in water and it was quite a job to keep everything dry. When I was through I scraped the mud off myself, changed, and went back next door to the office to see how the land lay—Captain Blanche told me to take it easy for a day or two and to get acquainted with the place and the people and suggested that since it was four o'clock Hartz might as well knock off and show me around.

The showing around started by a visit to the NCOs' mess which was sharing a huge marquee with the kitchen and stores. An essential visit for, according to an old Legion custom, a new-comer to the mess and the Company was expected to pay a few drinks all round. I knew most of the other NCOs in the Company so the ritual was accomplished without too much damage—the worst part of it was having to listen to the individual accounts of the cyclone. One had gone to bed naked and woke up to find his tent, clothes and bedding washed away, another had been bowled over and knocked flat into the river by a hogshead of wine and had only just been able to jerk free from the mud before he drowned, a third had salvaged the rum barrel just as it was floating away, the mess had been stinking on rum for three days after and so on. After a few drinks we went out again for a look round before the evening meal. I got an idea of the layout of the place, ate and then went off to bed. I was dog-tired and felt very much at sea. The change was abrupt enough for anybody.

The weather was fine and clear and there was a full moon shining, brightly enough to make a lamp unnecessary—even inside the sick-bay, which was just as well; there was no electricity and a candle near a bed would have brought all the mosquitoes in Cochinchina flocking around. I managed to get undressed, balanced on a couple of rocks so as not to get my feet wet and fell into bed with a sigh of relief.

As soon as I hit the bed I came out of it and straight into the water on the floor, at the same time loosing off a wavering yell of mingled fear and surprise. There was something in my bed which had felt like a snake a mile and a half long and I was allergic to snakes. Hartz, who was next door, came in with a flash lamp to ask what the devil was wrong. I had alerted most of the post with the yell I had let off. Unable to speak, I pointed shakily towards the bed and looked away. He flashed his lamp on the bed and began to laugh; after a while he pulled himself together and told me not to worry, it was only Mitzi—I was beginning to get a bit angry now the shock had passed and started to swear at him for being a damn fool—I knew perfectly well that it was no woman in my bed.

Getting generally acquainted. . . .

Hartz apologised, still laughing, and explained that Mitzi was a pet boa-constrictor belonging to Grauss, the sick-bay attendant. Grauss had been in the habit of putting her in the spare bed to keep out of the damp and must have forgotten her. Fortunately Grauss arrived just then and picked the brute out of my bed, waded across to his and put her there. I spent a very bad night. I soon got used to the beast, however, and so long as I didn't get closer than a couple of yards to her I finally became quite fond of boas. They make very peaceful pets.

My next few days were spent in acclimatising myself to the new rhythm of life and getting generally acquainted with the Company and the everyday routine which was different from that at HQ in almost every respect. To begin with there was only one officer there, the platoons were commanded by NCOs, and when the Captain was away it was one of us who had to take over. Secondly we were stuck miles away from any other form of European life. The nearest village or town was Tay Ninh, and the jungle which surrounded us was hostile from the moment we had lost sight of the post. On two sides the jungle was about fifteen yards away, and its furthest was barely a hundred yards off.

Every time I tackled Captain Blanche about getting down to work he put me off and said there was no hurry, told me to take things easy and relax for a little, suggested that I drop down to Tay Ninh for the day or took me off on tours of inspection of the work we had in hand and asked me to admire what he was doing. In the end I got fed up with my forced inactivity and started to take an increasing part in the daily patrols, and scouting expeditions with the platoons. All of which didn't settle the problem that Hartz was leaving fairly soon and that I would be taking over from him. After a week or so of bumbling around doing what I liked, I asked the Captain to put me into a platoon and suggested No. 2 where I had the most friends. That set him off. By the time he'd finished tearing a strip off me I found myself definitely assigned to take over from Hartz and for a while all went for the best in the best of worlds between the Captain and me.

Hartz and I were in no hurry for the official handing over of functions, and he was in even less of a hurry when I told of Lieutenant Dindon's warning before I left HQ. He himself had never countersigned the registers as his predecessor had been killed on a patrol and the Captain had taken over the Company's finances. The resulting mess was appalling and Hartz had but little idea of where the Company stood except that it was in the red. Even the unofficial Company kitty was almost empty. Normally the kitty should have been fairly prosperous. At Cau Chi the Company had done quite a bit of cattle rustling and several profitable *razzia* on villages just within the Viet zone and, right there at Suo Hiep, the Captain had managed to fix up a deal with a Caodai timber merchant who came daily to haul away the trees cut down by the men clearing the jungle. A happy solution for everybody—the Caodai got his wood and the men were saved the trouble of burning what they had cut down. The nigger in the woodpile, however, was a barmaid the Captain had picked up in Saigon and whom he went to see at least once a week—she seemed to be a very expensive hobby.

Chapter
16

CAPTAIN BLANCHE'S VISITS to Saigon were generally regarded as holidays by everyone in the post. Before leaving he put Sergeant Schiller in charge and, once his jeep had disappeared down the road in its accompanying cloud of dust, everybody knocked off for the day, except the platoon whose turn it was to guard and patrol the road. Naturally enough, the Captain always camouflaged his trips by cooking up some urgent official business which had called him to Battalion Headquarters, but all that Battalion HQ saw of him was the tail-end of the jeep scooting off towards Saigon. It was a reasonably foolproof system—we were far enough off the beaten track to present little interest for surprise visitors by passing brasshats and our local sector commander in Tay Ninh left us well alone.

The day of the Captain's second or third trip in mid-October, Hartz and I were sitting in the office-cum-officers' mess trying to decide whether or not to get some work done; it was about 10 a.m. and we weren't feeling very courageous. Suddenly we heard unaccustomed footsteps stamping along the log walk leading to the office and a very odd-looking figure swept in, tossed a quirt and a stetson into the only armchair and perched on the corner of the desk, having first slapped us on the back.

She, for it turned out to be a woman, never gave us time to

say a word and launched straight into a voluble enquiry as to the whereabouts of her dear little Captain, her greatest friend—the latter with a knowing leer—whom she must see immediately on a matter of the greatest importance. The whole in execrable broken French. I had had time to see that she was Annamite, fat, ugly as sin and dressed in blue jeans, checked shirt, cowboy boots and the stetson which was in the armchair. The effect was topped off by a pair of gold earrings the size of soup-plates, deep blue lipstick and a pair of outsize Colts strapped around her waist by two crossed cartridge belts, and stuck into the belts was a murderous-looking knife. She looked a bit like an Annamite version of Elsa Maxwell playing a Western.

Hartz and I were thunderstruck. The slap she had given me still made my back tingle and her voice was a husky baritone. Hartz came to the first and told her that the Captain was not there for the moment and asked what we could do for her. The reply was prompt and to the point. We could give her a drink, something straight and strong; she felt a little tired as she had been tramping around the jungle all the morning. Hartz looked across at me in despair, but I let him carry on, I hadn't come to sufficiently to be coherent. He would have killed me with the greatest pleasure but was forced to be polite. He asked her to sit down for a minute while he sent for something to drink. She rasped out a 'Thank you' and, stumping over to the Captain's camp-bed, pulled out the pillows, put them against the wall and settled down to wait for her drink. She was so short that her feet dangled inches off the ground. Hartz got one up on me then; instead of sending the orderly to fetch the drinks he went himself and left me alone with her.

For a few seconds I tried to think of some small-talk, then gave up and asked her what she was doing round those parts, pointing out that it wasn't a very healthy spot to choose for morning walks. She let off a hoarse chuckle and said that she was scared of nothing, of nobody, slapping her Colts as she said so. Then she added that all the jungle round there belonged to her and that she had been checking on how much timber we had felled and how much the contractor had hauled out.

She trusted nobody and preferred to see for herself what was going on. She had dropped in to see the Captain—such a dear man, she said—to ask him to send out an extra platoon to guard the men she was going to send in to cut out the choice trees. He was so understanding and every time he dropped round to see her at Tay Ninh—a heavy wink—he always agreed to do what he could to help her.

She then started to assure me that she was a generous and open-hearted soul who knew how to reward services rendered. Her husband, a Caodai Colonel, was old and tired but so understanding, and would certainly be delighted if I cared to come round to lunch one day, even if he wasn't there. I was mighty relieved when Hartz appeared with a bottle of brandy, ice and soda. I had no ambition to take over from Captain Blanche, for whom I was beginning to feel a growing admiration—between his barmaid and his pistol-packing momma he must have had his hands full.

Hartz, who saw that the going had been heavy, poured me out a stiff one and I was so grateful that I was almost ready to forgive him for having abandoned me. Our guest kept up a running stream of explanations about herself, her soul and her money for about half-an-hour, by when she had finished half the bottle of brandy—Hartz and I had shared the other half. We were both hoping that she would decide to go now that the bottle was finished. I made a move towards the desk and started to apologise for having to get back to work. Hartz began the same manœuvre. Nothing doing; she intended to wait till the Captain came back for lunch and she was sure he wouldn't mind if we kept her company.

It was none of her business where he had gone and elementary security precautions kept us from telling her that he was down in Saigon for the day. We were stuck, and short of picking her up and throwing her out there was no way of getting rid of her—

and the way she was loaded up with weapons neither of us felt like taking the risk. Also we knew that the Captain had made a deal on the timber and we couldn't afford to spoil the whole thing if she was, as she maintained, the source of money for the Company.

The half-bottle of brandy seemed to have had no effect on her whatsoever and she soon asked for another drink to while away the time—it was only eleven-thirty and she knew that the Captain —the dear boy—never lunched before half-past twelve.

It was my turn for a breather and I shot out to get some more liquor before Hartz had time to move. On my way to the mess I dropped in to see Schiller and told him what had happened to us. He laughed like a drain and then suggested that perhaps the best thing to do was to invite her to eat with us in the mess. Once lunch was over, we could say that the Captain had, undoubtedly, been detained at Tay Ninh, by the Sector Commander. That ought to be enough to get her off to Tay Ninh in a hurry. Schiller had seen her arrive in an armoured jeep, but hadn't been close enough to see who it was. He went off to the mess together and while he made arrangements for her to eat with us I got another bottle of brandy and headed back to the office.

I got back to find Hartz looking slightly groggy. He must have been fighting off the same proposition that she had put to me. It made me feel a lot better. We finished that bottle in the same manner as the first—she had half and Hartz and I shared the other, but whereas he and I were definitely woolly, she hadn't turned a hair.

While we were downing the second bottle I told had her that the NCOs had invited her to lunch with them in their mess and that if the Captain turned up in time he was invited as well. The bottle finished, she intimated that she was ready for lunch and led the way out of the office down to the marquee. Hartz and I staggered down the log walk after her. We managed to reach dry land without falling into the quagmire, though we both had several near misses. In the mess Schiller and the others were waiting for us and were obviously well primed, by Schiller, as to our guest's eccentricities. Our pistol-packing momma, however, had the best of us. After downing incredible quantities of wine and brandy, a huge meal and several of the Tay Ninh officers' reputations, she reacted according to plan. When Schiller suggested that the Captain had been kept to lunch by the Sector Commander she disappeared in her jeep at sixty m.p.h. to rejoin her dear boy. As the final swirl of dust settled to the ground we were still trying to find out what had hit us. She had put away twice as much drink as any of us and had left as fresh as a daisy, while we were having our work cut out to stay on our feet.

Hartz, Schiller and I tottered off to bed and I don't think the others were long in doing the same. If the Viet had wanted the post that afternoon they could have walked in and kept it for all we cared. I came to round five o'clock and when I opened my eyes the first thing that I saw was Mitzi looking at me from Grauss's bed with a cold unwinking stare. Luckily I had met her before; even so, it was unnerving. I got up, showered and dressed and wandered down to the mess, where I found Schiller looking just the way I felt. Naturally enough we started talking about the Caodai woman, we couldn't remember her name, it was too complicated, so from then on she was known as the pistol-packer. The others drifted in one by one and in the general discussion of the day's events we all came to the conclusion that the Captain was a genuine hero—a man who would stop at nothing to save his company from financial disaster; everybody knew that something had gone wrong with the accounts, though nobody knew exactly what.

By the time we had finished the evening meal, dusk was already beginning to fall and the Captain had still not arrived. Normally he got back from his Saigon trips about six, and we began to get a bit worried—Schiller especially so. He had no particular desire to be responsible for the post overnight in case we had a night attack. In the event of an attack he would have quite enough to do controlling his platoon, let alone the whole Company. As the time went by we all became increasingly nervous, and when, about nine o'clock we heard ragged firing in the distance Schiller decided to keep the Company on the alert. The firing had come from down the road, in the direction of the nearest Caodai post, and he was afraid that it might have meant an ambush for the Captain and an attack for us. Nothing happened, however, and by midnight we came to the conclusion that the Captain must have had either a breakdown or some reason to stay in Saigon overnight. Schiller called off the alert and those of us who weren't on duty that night turned in. But not for long.

About one in the morning we were all woken up by the sentry in the tower, who was yelling his head off. He shouted that he could see headlights coming down the road and that, whatever it was, it was coming fast. Most of the Company got up and clustered round the entrance of the barbed-wire defences, taking little notice of Schiller who was trying to get them to spread out a bit in case it was some trick of the Viet.

As it approached, we could see it was a jeep and that it was coming down on the post like a bat out of hell. Within a few seconds the jeep drew up in a cloud of dust, the Captain's head poked round the windscreen and he asked what the hell we were waiting for to open the gates. The gates swung open and the jeep leapt forward at full speed, then skidded to a stop, just opposite the log walk which led into the office. The Captain's driver staggered out of the back of the jeep and got to the ground looking dazed and shaken. The Captain, after racing the engine for a bit, switched off the contact and got out in his turn. As soon as his feet touched the ground he fell over flat on his face. Schiller and I picked him up, dusted him off and propped him up against the jeep, but he fell over again, this time on his back. We got him up again and put him back in the jeep in the hope that he could still sit up, at least. During the whole performance he hadn't stopped laughing, a beautiful, unquenchable drunken laugh. Hartz, meanwhile, had managed to keep the men away and there was only a handful of us there to see the state he was in. The driver had settled down against the rear wheel and was fast asleep.

Finally the Captain stopped laughing and started to tell us what he was laughing about. He had been on his way back and had reached Tay Ninh about five o'clock. When he got to the branch road he found the pistol-packer lying in wait for him. She had found out that he had been to Saigon and had started to raise hell. To keep her quiet he had gone to her house for a few drinks and, once there, she had told him that she had been to see him at the Company; she also told him how she had stayed to lunch with all those dear NCOs in their mess and how all the poor boys had drunk too much trying to amuse her. He found all that very funny. When he had laughed himself out we tried to get him across the log walk to put him to bed. But there was nothing doing, he insisted that he commanded the Company and could go to bed when he liked. What we needed was something to cheer us up. Then he turned to Schiller and told him to get some champagne opened up in the mess—he wanted us all to have a drink with him. There was nothing to do but go and have it in the hopes that he might pass out there. Once he had reached the mess and we had all had a drink we suggested bed again.

Tired, were we? What we needed was something to wake us up. With that he staggered out and started roaring orders for everybody to get to action stations at the double. When the men were in place he ordered a rapid and general fire with all arms. The men couldn't have asked for anything better. For five minutes there was unholy uproar as everything let loose at the same time—mortars, machine-guns, rifles and grenades being fired in all directions. The racket must have sobered him up a bit for as soon as the first lull came he ordered the 'Cease fire' and insisted on a final round in the mess, during which we had all our time cut out dissuading him from ordering a general sortie from the post to attack the Viet. We managed to get him to understand that it was the Viet's night off, they had even let him come down the road unescorted without attacking him. 'That's right,' said he. 'Damn nice people—they know what they're up against when I'm around.' Between the pistol-packer and her dear Captain we had had enough for the day, and as soon as the Captain disappeared, we made for bed.

We kept radio contact with the Tay Ninh HQ, but only once a day at seven in the morning. The next morning the radio operator woke me up to say that a message had come through asking for an urgent report on the action we had had that night. Tay Ninh said that heavy firing had been heard in our area and wanted to know what had happened. They were going to call back in half an hour. I struggled out of bed and went off to wake up the Captain. It was hopeless. He was flat out, sleeping like a log, and after twenty minutes of useless efforts I gave up. I woke Hartz instead, and the two of us sat down to cook up a report on a night alert, followed by an attack by the Viet who had been driven off after a five-minute engagement in which all arms had been used. We added that our losses were nil and the Viet losses were unknown as they had disappeared with their wounded. Estimated strength of the Viet: two companies. When Tay Ninh called back the radio operator gave them the report, then came back to warn Hartz and me that a written confirmation was expected at Tay Ninh later in the day.

The Captain came to about midday. As soon as he had brushed his teeth and had a little coffee well laced with brandy we told him the bad news. He had forgotten that he had ordered all arms to fire the night before, but finally got round to remembering and decided that under the circumstances Hartz and I had saved the day. The only thing he changed in the report was to cut down the attacking force from two companies to one. To thank us he let Hartz, Schiller and me borrow the jeep to deliver the report and have a drink in town.

Chapter
17

LIFE AT SUO HIEP, however, was not all beer and skittles and afternoons with the pistol-packer. By November the Viet had recovered from the shock of the cyclone and had increased their activity considerably.

Apart from the actual construction of the post the surrounding jungle had to be cut down, the road de-mined every morning and guarded all day, and patrols had to keep moving round the area to offset any surprise attack. The total lack of comfort, the heat, water rationing and a hundred other pinpricks all combined to increase the fatigue of the men, who were already worn out by their day-and-night activity. It was rare for a day to pass without an alert or an incident or some kind, and most nights the Viet loosed off a shot or two or an odd mortar shell to keep us on the *qui vive* and to cut down our sleep.

The first serious incident came on the first of November. Number 3 platoon was out on the routine road-opening patrol, checking the road for mines. They had just picked up the trace of a mine when they fell into an ambush. It took them twenty minutes to fight their way out of it and cost them three wounded. A couple of days later it was Number 1 platoon's turn. They were out on a reconnaissance patrol and had left the post just after the midday meal. It was a good time to go out as nearly everybody, including the Viet, observed siesta and it was sometimes possible to surprise a group of Viet before they had time to get away. The platoon had been gone about half an hour when we heard heavy machine-gun firing coming from the direction it had taken. After a short lull we could pick out the sound of the platoon's Bren and tommy-guns being answered back again by the machine-guns and what sounded like light mortar and recoil-less cannon fire. It was obvious that they had run into serious trouble. What was equally and tragically obvious was that we couldn't send more than one platoon to cover them while they broke off the action. We had one platoon out on the road protecting the coolies and the traffic and only one would be left to protect the post in case the Viet sprang a surprise attack.

Meanwhile the firing kept up its intensity and within three minutes the standby platoon was making off at the double, the men buckling on their equipment as they ran, the Captain in the lead and myself, getting hopelessly outdistanced,' taking up the rear. We cut through the underbrush as best we could and took the minimum of precautions; with all the racket from the firing ahead it was very doubtful if anyone could have heard our approach. It took us some fifteen minutes of hard going to reach Number 1 platoon, which had sheltered behind a bank. The other side of the bank lay open country and abandoned paddy-fields, the Viet were on and behind the dikes in the paddy-fields and were trying to surround the platoon. We opened fire with everything we had and under the cover of it Number 1 platoon fell back. We continued to leap-frog until we were out of range, then cut on back to the post as fast as we could. It was not very fast, as the first bursts of Viet fire had wounded six men, two of them seriously. Schiller, who was commander of Number 1 platoon, said that the Viet had been at least two companies strong and seemed to have been on a training manœuvre of some kind. The men wounded had all been in the lead group and had been knocked out by the same machine-gun. It had taken the

Sixty Cambodian souls.

Viet several minutes to swing round their other heavy stuff, by which time he had manœuvred his platoon under shelter behind the bank. He hadn't had the necessary fire power, however, to make the Viet keep their heads down long enough to let him get the platoon out of range.

On the way back I managed to spike my leg on a bamboo—not much more than a scratch, which took months to heal and crippled me for weeks, though not enough to keep me from hobbling around my normal duties.

Nine men knocked out in a week were heavy losses for the Company, especially added to the men who went down with dysentery and malaria, and we were shortly reduced to an overall marching effective of sixty out of a total effective of a hundred and twenty. In spite of urgent requests for more men we rarely got more than two a week, and it just meant double the effort for everybody.

Late in October the Sector Commander had agreed to build a small heavily fortified post to guard our rear. It was placed about a mile from our post, in the direction of Tay Ninh, next to a small stream and a bridge which the Viet were constantly mining. If ever they had blown it up we would have been completely cut off from all outside help. In a couple of weeks the smaller post was finished, surrounded by a maze of barbed wire about fifty feet wide and manned by a platoon of thirty Cambodian auxiliaries—which meant about sixty Cambodian souls. The married Cambodian auxiliaries rarely moved without their wives and children and at least ten of that lot were married. In charge of the post was a Sergeant Miku from our company seconded by one Légionnaire. Theoretically the post was impregnable to everything except howitzer fire or aerial bombardment.

On November 10th, a week to the day after Number 1 platoon's affray, life was much the same as ever. Just before dusk Sergeant Miku left the mess to get back to his post. He had come up for a beer, as he did most evenings. The rest of us had supper and went

M   177

either to bed or, if we were on guard, went the rounds. The sky had clouded over and it was a dark heavy night. I was reading in bed when a fantastic explosion blew out my petrol lamp, and knocked me on to the floor where I met Mitzi—she must have been knocked out of her box. Within seconds I was outside to see what was going on. A heavy mortar shell had burst in the middle of the post, knocked most of the roofing off, but had hurt nobody. The first shell was followed by a lot of others, which fell outside the camp, and sustained bursts of heavy machine-gun fire. The Captain was up in the tower yelling at the men not to fire till he gave the order. Finally he spotted the corner from which the Viet were firing and ordered our machine-guns and mortars to answer. After a few bursts he ordered a 'Cease fire'.

The Viet seemed to have had the same idea. All was quiet round the post, but we could hear and see the flashes of heavy firing coming from the post by the bridge. The Captain told me to try to contact Miku on the short-range set—in case of trouble he had orders to have someone permanently on his set. I tried for half an hour and later for odd spells throughout the night, but I couldn't get an answer from him. The firing continued and from time to time there were heavy explosions; there was no doubt about it, the Viet were launching a full-scale attack. We had to wait till daylight before doing anything, however. We couldn't have risked sending less than three platoons, and if we did that it was a safe bet that the Viet who had peppered us would take the post. To keep us aware of their presence they lobbed in a mortar shell from time to time and fired odd shots from the surrounding jungle. All that we could do to help Miku was to bombard the terrain outside his post with our heavy mortar and the mobile seventy-five on loan from Tay Ninh, but as we had no radio contact with him we didn't know what effect it had and we couldn't direct our fire.

We spent a terrible night of frustration and despair, unable to make a sortie, knowing that aerial intervention was out of the question and that the Tay Ninh would have had to send a battalion at least, which they didn't have. It was plain hell sitting there, completely impotent, waiting for the dawn to break.

The battle down at Miku's post lasted all night, and when dawn finally broke the Captain sent two platoons to see what was going on. They kept off the road for fear of mines and, when they arrived within a hundred yards, they had to stop and fight it out with the Viet rearguard. The latter soon broke off, however, and disappeared. When they reached what was left of the post they found a heap of smoking ruins and a handful of Cambodians under the command of a Cambodian sergeant. Miku and the Légionnaire had been killed at the very beginning, when the Viet had blown up part of the building with plastic. For the rest of the night the Cambodians had been fighting off the Viet, with grenades and bayonets, and had managed to prevent them from getting beyond the main entrance. They had fought doubly hard on account of their women and children, some of whom were still alive. In all there were sixteen survivors amongst the men, of whom all but six were badly wounded; ten of the women had been killed outright when the post blew up and about the same number wounded. Two hours later when the road was opened we took the dead, the wounded and the survivors to Tay Ninh.

The destruction of the post had the effect of an electric shock on the General Staff at Saigon. We had radioed a brief summary and by late in the morning a full report had been sent off. The following morning a couple of Generals with their twin cortèges of experts and aides arrived at the main post of Suo Hiep, escorted by a fleet of armoured cars and several truck-loads of heavily armed men. For an hour or so they stumped around our unfinished post making intelligent noises, suggestions and counter-suggestions. They came to the conclusion that the post should never have been built in the middle of the only hollow for miles around, clearing or no clearing. Captain Blanche managed to get in a sly crack to the effect that he thought they were quite right, but that the site had been chosen by the Generals' engineering experts.

There was a short and very shocked silence and the subject was hastily changed. They decided that they had seen all that was necessary of the post and asked the Captain to go along with them to the ruins of the small post by the river. They climbed into their respective cars and jeeps and the convoy lumbered off down the road with Captain Blanche in the lead.

He came back jubilant. Before leaving, the senior of the two Generals had taken him to one side and asked him what he needed to get the post finished and defendable. Without hesitating he had asked for half a dozen bulldozers, the men necessary to guard them at night and assure their safety during the day, and for at least one good commando of auxiliaries to help with the patrol and general security duties of the post. Within a week his request had been fulfilled, including the commando. The bulldozers were heaven-sent for clearing the brush and tangled jungle growth round the post and along the road. In a few days the post took on an entirely different aspect. We had clear vision for nearly a hundred yards around us and driving down the road was beginning to lose some of its horror. The Viet, however, took a poor view of the whole business and redoubled their road-mining and early morning ambush efforts.

To make sure that nothing went wrong down at the small post while it was being rebuilt the Captain had sent Schiller and his platoon as garrison. He had also managed to get our road-opening distances reduced to ease the strain on the Company. The new routine was for a platoon to go down as far as Schiller's post in the morning and wait there until the Tay Ninh armoured groups arrived from the other direction. For the next few weeks there was rarely a day when they arrived before eleven in the morning. It took them a good four hours to make the twelve miles owing to mines and an occasional ambush. The Caodai posts along the way were of no help as they were either too scared or too well bribed to move until the armoured patrols had gone by. The only people who seemed to be able to pass with impunity were the pistol-packer's wood-cutters and their trucks. They never had a truck mined while we were there. The pistol-packer explained that away by slapping her Colts and announcing that the Viet knew who they had to deal with if anything happened to her men and material.

None the less we went on having a steady driblet of casualties, and as the Company was shrinking as the weeks went by the strain was beginning to tell on the men. In our mess we could make at least a semblance of relaxing; for the men there was nowhere to go and for all comfort a bottle or two of lukewarm beer. What little native population there was was irrevocably unfriendly and the only contact with the outside world was the provision truck which went down to Saigon five times a fortnight.

In spite of the heat, the discomfort and the drudgery of our existence, there was one event which all of us looked forward to and that was the visit of the sector's welfare worker. An ugly little woman in her late thirties, she had come out from France as a volunteer and, unlike the majority of her colleagues, she had thrown herself wholeheartedly into her job. She didn't give a damn how far away or how dangerous the different posts were and she somehow managed to get to the most isolated of them at least once a month. Her main job was to settle the private worries and troubles of the men, but at the same time took a lively interest in all that affected our lives and did her best to smooth out minor official troubles when she could. When she wasn't touring round the posts she was visiting our sick and wounded in the hospitals, and her integrity and simplicity were such that she received the maximum help and encouragement on all levels. She had won the men over from the start by her complete indifference to rank, race or creed, and by her ready acceptance of hospitality, be it in the men's canteens or the NCOs' and officers' messes.

Five days after Miku's post had been destroyed she was due for her monthly visit. A sure sign was the unusual number of freshly shaved faces and clean shirts to be seen about the post. By midday she hadn't arrived and it was easy to read the disappointment of the men in their studious unconcern. Around two o'clock we heard a dull thud in the distance and a few minutes later Schiller called through on his radio to say that a mine had gone off half a mile from his post and that he had sent a patrol to investigate. He called back a quarter of an hour later and in a tear-choked voice told us that a jeep had been blown up. In it were a Captain from Tay Ninh, the social worker and two men as escort. They had all been killed.

The news flashed round the post and the effect was terrible. Groups of men everywhere muttering oaths to keep themselves from bawling like children. It was so loathsomely unnecessary— why she of all people? The Captain sent off a truck and an escort to take the bodies back to Tay Ninh and there was nearly a pitched battle between the men. Every single one wanted to escort her back to Tay Ninh. With her death we had all lost a little part of ourselves and a great deal of the hope that formed a part of the everyday courage. We were angry, but not so much against the Viet as against the stupidity of the whole Indochinese war, which wasn't a war; fighting an enemy we rarely saw for an ideal we had all but lost sight of.

The funeral ceremonies were fixed for two days later. By careful calculation the Captain had been able to delegate about twenty of us to go down to Saigon and still leave the post with enough men. We arrived to find that every unit in the Sector had managed to send along representatives. The square outside the church was crammed with Légionnaires, auxiliaries and North Africans, and there must have been nearly five hundred of us without counting the staff officers and different women's services. The entrance to the church was a solid bank of wreaths and the coffins were completely smothered in them. The church itself was too small to hold everybody present, so it had been reserved for the officers and the women in uniform. The rest of us waited outside during the service. Once it was over the coffins were carried out and she and the Captain were placed side by side; behind them, at a respectful distance, were placed the coffins of the two soldiers who had been with them. A hush fell over the crowd as a General stepped forward to deliver the funeral oration, in the course of which he paid tribute to the place she had held in our lives. By the time he had finished it was becoming hard to hear what he had to say through the trumpeting of all the noses which were being blown suspiciously hard.

When the General had finished the bugler sounded the Last Post, the two soldiers' coffins were carried away to the cemetery, discreetly followed by a handful of their friends.

Her coffin and the Captain's were loaded on to two trucks, the wreaths followed and the two trucks set off at walking pace. Our delegation had been given the honour of forming her last escort, so we boarded the truck, in which she lay, to guard her coffin. We had no idea of where we were going. Half an hour later we arrived outside a warehouse on the outskirts of Saigon, in the dock area. The trucks stopped outside the warehouse and we all piled off, feeling a bit lost and stupid, wondering what to do with ourselves. We were far from the church, both in space and time, and for most of us the incident was closed. After a short wait a man in dungarees came out of the warehouse chewing on a sandwich and told us to bring the coffins inside. Eight men picked up each coffin and carried them in. The rest of us trooped in after them, still uncertain as to the procedure to follow.

For a moment or two it was hard to see anything at all after the blinding light of the sun. As we became accustomed to the darkness we could see a stack of something rising up to the roof of the warehouse, and when our eyes finally got into focus we realised that it was a stack of coffins. The man in dungarees came up and told us that they were all waiting for shipment back to France and, as an afterthought, added that they were arranged according to rank. At the time it didn't sound odd in the least. Once the men had put the coffins down we turned to leave, but at the same moment the bugler, who had come with us, began to sound the Last Post again. The notes swept up to the roof of the warehouse and came rolling back, amplified and eerie. When he blew the final note we were all openly and unashamedly in tears—not because she was dead but because we had all been far back into our lives and felt terribly and irrevocably alone.

As we left the warehouse the man in dungarees came up and gave us a receipt, then pulled his half-finished sandwich from his pocket and took a bite of it.

Chapter
18

SLOWLY BUT SURELY the post began to take shape and by the beginning of December the outer walls and defences were finished and the shells of the buildings completed. We moved the NCOs' mess and the stores under cover, though the platoons remained under canvas until the post was completed, to be near the outer defences in case of attack.

To inaugurate the mess we decided to invite one or two outsiders from Tay Ninh to come over and spend the night with us. By common consent we picked the sector commander's second-in-command. He was our immediate superior and in some sort controlled our operational activity. Our intentions were to try and persuade him to organise a little operation in the neighbourhood. We were all fed up with rotting away inside the post and its immediate surroundings, being sniped at with never a chance to hit back. He was a pleasant man and, even though he was a regular army Major, he easily forgot his rank when he dropped into the mess for a drink. The other two guests we asked were sergeants who commanded the armoured car patrols which opened the roads as far as the small post. They were both Moroccans, but not so fanatically Mahommedan that they wouldn't have a drink. One of them in particular was a very popular man in the Company. He had organised a private brothel in Tay Ninh, the girls were attractive and he made a special rate for our company whenever any of us got a chance of spending the day in town.

We picked a Saturday for the party as, by common consent, all work was automatically suspended on Sundays and even Saturday afternoons were comparatively calm. The Major agreed and arrived by jeep escorted by the armoured car patrol, which was to spend the night at the post and start its road opening from the wrong end in the morning. Distraction in the mess was limited to drinking and a gramophone with a few cracked records, so ultimately it boiled down to just drinking.

We put the Major to bed at four in the morning. Captain Blanche had been able to get himself to bed about three, and at eight we lifted the Major out of bed and poured him into his jeep. We later learned that he wasn't seen around Tay Ninh barracks for three whole days; on the fourth, looking very pale behind an enormous pair of sun-glasses, he had been seen taking the air. He dropped down to see us at the end of the week and told the Captain that he had organised a nice little operation for us! A Viet deserter had appeared at Tay Ninh and had disclosed the whereabouts of a Viet arms factory in a village a few miles from our post. He gave the Captain all the necessary details and said that he was sending along another company which would be under the Captain's orders, to strengthen our effective. Zero hour was to be six the next morning; the extra company would arrive that evening. When we asked him to drink to the success of the operation he shied out of the mess like a skittish colt and made a dash for his jeep. As he drove away he shouted out that he would send the Colonel down for a drink in a couple of days. We were none too sure who was being threatened, the Colonel or ourselves.

At six the next morning the Captain took off with three platoons from our Company and the other Company. Schiller and I stayed behind in the post with the commando and the remaining platoon; my leg was still in such a state that I could barely walk a hundred yards. The Captain had taken a walkie-talkie along to keep in contact with the post and to direct the other companies; after an hour, however, we lost contact and switched off. Even if they ran into trouble there was nothing we could do but warn Tay Ninh and they wouldn't be able to do much more than make encouraging noises. Around five in the afternoon the sentinel up in the watch-tower shouted down that ragged volleys were being fired in the distance. Schiller told him to listen and count the next volley. He counted three, which was the distress signal, so Schiller told him to fire three bursts of the machine-gun in reply. A quarter of an hour later we heard a series of three volleys a good deal closer, so Schiller decided to send out a group with stretchers to meet them. When the companies finally broke into the clearing we could see that they must have had a pretty tough time. The men were scarcely able to walk. As they straggled across to the post we saw the stretchers come into the clearing; the seven stretchers Schiller had sent out were loaded and there were others following behind. The Captain came in as dead beat as the men and we heard what had happened.

It had been the old, classic story. After a three-hour struggle through the jungle and brush they had broken into open country and come across a small village. Everything was quiet and peaceful and the villagers just looked at them. When asked if they had seen any Viet around there, they just shrugged, nodded 'No' and turned their back to whatever they were doing. A couple of yards from the village they went into the brush again and came across the river, which was the landmark they were heading for, and shortly after picked up the track which led to the arms factory village. There had been a brief halt while the Captain made the platoons get into position and they advanced with the greatest possible caution. They had just sighted the roof-tops of what was undoubtedly the village when a warning shot rang out, a string of remote control mines went off and all hell broke loose. There was nothing to be done but turn back. They had already a dozen wounded and two dead, they were at least four hours from the post and they hadn't a hope in hell of getting nearer the arms factory without suffering very heavy casualties, with no chance of any outside or air help. They hadn't even been able to fire at anything, and never so much as saw the Viet, who were all too well camouflaged.

An impression that everything we were doing, even building the post, was of the utmost futility began to settle on the company; and the impression, like a leech, sucked away what little vitality was left in the men. Dysentery, malaria and general fatigue made the situation even more critical. Finally, in mid-December the Captain made an urgent request for an immediate and large reinforcement to be sent along. He pointed out that, with his reduced numbers and increasing sickness rate, the post was rapidly becoming untenable in the case of an attack. The Viet had at least two battalions of regional troops in the immediate vicinity and he no longer had the manpower to send out even reconnaissance patrols, knowing that if a patrol ran into trouble he would be unable to send more men to the rescue. He also pointed out that the Company had been there for nearly four months and that, owing to the shortage of coolie labour, only one-third of the work had been accomplished in two-thirds of the allocated time.

The answer he got was amazing. He was told that we would be relieved by a company of auxiliaries at the end of the month as GHQ Saigon had decided to suspend all work except that necessary for the completion of the post! Our feelings were very mixed when we heard the news. We were at the same time disgusted at having been sold down the river and wild with delight of leaving that particular hell-hole. Even though ours was to do or die and not to reason why, we still couldn't help letting disgust get the upper hand. For a few days the conversations in the mess were particularly bitter against the politico-military clique in Saigon who controlled our lives and the price of rubber at the same time and in the same breath.

The Captain decided that our departure deserved a mammoth celebration and, as Christmas was approaching, chose the day before Christmas Eve. Just how he did it we never knew, but he invited every single one of our hierarchic superiors, right up to the Zone Commander and including our Regimental Colonel, and they all agreed to come along. By the time he had finished inviting everybody we found that we had a hundred and twenty guests against the eighty-odd members of the company, and the eighty included the sick and wounded well enough to be let out of hospital on a twenty-four hour pass. With a week to go till Christmas we had our work cut out to get everything ready. We had nothing in the post except a few odd plates and cutlery, which made the writing up of the list of essentials a great deal easier. Once we had established the list, the next problem was money. At the very last moment the Captain found that the coffers were bare—he just didn't have the money to get all we would need. By dint of browbeating the tradesmen in Saigon we finally arranged sufficient credit and brought back a truckload of food, drink and decorations. Meanwhile the Captain had been busy and had persuaded the Sector Commander to put a battalion of auxiliaries and three patrols of armoured cars around the post and along the road to protect the guests. His main argument had been that seven Colonels, four Majors, innumerable Captains and other ranks were too valuable to leave for the Viet to pick up like apples off a tree.

By the time the appointed day came round we were all completely worn out and nobody in the Company understood just what had got into the Captain. It all seemed like the hell of a lot of fuss and hard work for nothing. According to his plans, the guests were to begin arriving about three o'clock and wouldn't leave till nine or ten the next morning, which upset the men quite a bit. They didn't see why so much good liquor should go down the throats of outsiders and we had an appalling job keeping them away from the crates of wine, beer, champagne, aperitifs and brandy. Most of the drinks were destined for the trestles set up inside the post, but we couldn't put the bottles on the tables till the sun went down a bit.

The first guests to arrive gave us the clue to the Captain's idea of staging the party: he wanted to show off his latest conquest. Escorted by two armoured cars, an enormous limousine swept up to the post driven by a fat, sweaty and definitely black-market type. Out of the back stepped two overdressed, overpainted visions of a soldier's Saturday night. They were the Captain's barmaid and her girl friend. The man behind the wheel was the 'friend' of both the girls and was a Saigon drinking crony of the Captain's.

For the occasion the Captain's bedroom-office-mess-Company office had been divided in two by stringing a blanket across a wire. The Captain and his paramour had barely had time to disappear into his half when the pistol-packer came roaring up in her jeep, unescorted, but this time with a little silk dress and high-heeled shoes as a background for the inevitable Colts and quirt. She parked her jeep, got out and went striding into the post, slapping her leg with the quirt as she went. Hartz and I, hoping for a showdown, whipped into our half of the office and waited. We weren't disappointed, either. The pistol-packer had a remarkable power of expressing herself in French and, by the time she had finished with the Captain and his barmaid, we knew a lot of highly original ways of insulting somebody's parents right back to the seventh generation. When she had finished the pistol-packer knocked the blanket back and came into our half of the room. She sat herself squarely on the desk, let out a loud 'Ouff' of relief and asked for a brandy. It sounded like a promising start to the festivities. We saw the Captain a bit later. He laughed his head off and told us not to take any notice, that it was of no importance. During the rest of the afternoon the guests kept arriving until by sundown the last jeep-load of brass arrived and the official merry-making began.

From then on I had little time to watch the proceedings. I had been appointed majordomo and general supervisor of the party and had my hands full seeing that the men who were serving served, instead of eating and drinking what they were meant to be passing around. It was the first and I hope the last time I have ever had to control a meal for two hundred people. On the whole everything went fairly smoothly and what undoubtedly helped was the regimental band playing appropriate music in the background. The Captain had a stroke of genius when he thought of asking the band along—it drowned the majority of the wolf-whistles and bawdy cracks about the women; and the cracks came from men of whom the majority hadn't seen a woman of any colour, the pistol-packer apart, for weeks. Once the eating was done with there was a spate of speeches from the various Colonels present, who all said so nearly the same things that we wondered, afterwards, if they didn't pass the same set of notes along between themselves. The theme was that we were wonderful men doing a wonderful job and that, as good Légion-naires, we all knew we would win the good fight, even at the cost of our own lives: in which case we would have a grand time in the heaven reserved for the Legion talking about good old times with those who had gone before us.

During the speeches I had time to look around a bit and noticed that most of the others felt the way I did about the noble sentiments of the speakers. It took them about an hour to boost our morale and then we got down to the more serious business of proposing toasts. The toasting put everybody back into fine fettle and I had a renewed rush of actively supervising the replacement of the empty bottles by full ones. A delicate business, as most of the servers were half-seas over.

The Captain, when he felt that the right moment had come, stood up and asked for silence. He had important news to an-nounce to us, but first of all he would like to thank, in our name, our distinguished guests—a bow to the Colonels, who looked suitably embarrassed—for the pleasure it gave us to be honoured by their presence. He stopped there and had a drink before going on to the important news. The latter was that he had the pleasure to tell us that a well-known French star, Mlle Yvette—the barmaid, who seemed thrilled to have so many men look at her at the same time—had agreed to sing for us; also she had accepted his request to adopt the Company—a stunned silence—which made him feel that it was an opportune moment to ask the Colonel commanding the Regiment to make her an honorary Légionnaire. That really threw a jolt into us, as being an honorary Légionnaire was the privilege of certain Generals or visiting statesmen who had done something for or with the Legion. The Colonel, thoroughly embarrassed, got to his feet and made a perfect procrastination speech which made it sound as though it were an honour to be refused. Fortunately everybody, the Captain and the Colonel included, had been drinking for an hour or two and the incident wasn't taken any too seriously.

Amidst wild applause, Mlle Yvette got up and launched into a passable torch-song, which was well received, and then into a series of community songs which were a great success, her voice being drowned by those of the men. It was then well past midnight and I was so dead beat that I staggered off to lie down for a bit. I went straight off to sleep and though I was woken up all through the night by odd drunks staggering in and falling into my bed, I managed to keep the latter to myself till I woke up for good, with a splitting head, about five in the morning.

The racket going on outside was terrific, so I got up to go and have a look. It was stupendous. The first sight that met my eyes was that of the Colonel commanding the Zone having his nose punched by a Légionnaire because he had finished the last drops in a bottle. The Légionnaire then hauled another bottle out of his pocket—local brandy, from the look of it—and forced an enormous dose down the Colonel's throat to prove that there were no ill feelings between them. The poor Colonel, who was already passably high, looked ready to pass out for good. I went over to the trestles to get a drink and on the way ran into a couple of our sergeants who had collared the Colonel commanding the sector and were trying to teach him how to sing a German

Lieder. Every time he got a note wrong they made him have a drink to oil his throat; he looked very dazed and very happy. On all sides it was the same. The Company had gone berserk. An officer was no sooner spotted than he was collared and, for one reason or another, damn well obliged to down a drink. The women had fortunately withdrawn themselves from circulation. By six I was as high as a steeple myself and was busily reorganising a road-opening patrol, to be formed uniquely of Colonels and Majors. Luckily, every time I got three or four together the others had gone off to open another bottle.

Sometime round eight a few other NCOs of the Company and I were in the mess together trying to drink some coffee and we decided to start putting all of them into their jeeps and cars. We felt like having a nice cosy little session all on our own for a change. But it wasn't till ten that we saw the last of them off, closely followed by the Captain and Mlle Yvette, whom he was taking back to Saigon. He didn't want her to get scared on the way back. Schiller took over and the post went to sleep—well protected by the battalion of auxiliaries who were staying on till five in the afternoon.

At the post-mortem we held that evening we reckoned that it would take them all quite a while to forget their night in an advanced outpost threatened by the Viet. Christmas must have been a red-letter day for them.

Chapter
19

OUR NEW DESTINATION had been kept secret and it wasn't until New Year's Eve, the day of our departure, that we found out our true destination. The wildest rumours had been flying around and all of them proved to be wrong—they had ranged from our being sent off to the imperial palace at Dalat as Bao Dai's personal guard to being trained as a special airborne unit for rapid intervention. The truth was far more prosaic. We were to instal ourselves in the heart of a 'Rubber Empire', one of the biggest in the world, for a few weeks rest and at the same time try to dissuade the Viet from sabotaging the plantations by ringing the rubber trees—ringing consisted of bleeding the trees by cutting an inch-deep band of bark round the lower part of the tree trunks. It was a favourite pastime of the Viet.

We handed the post over to the relieving troops early in the morning; they were auxiliaries under native command and arrived with their wives, children and household chattels. They managed to look more like a circus on the move than part of an army, and didn't seem in the least thrilled at the idea of taking over. Their greatest preoccupation was to know how far from the post they could go in safety. When they learnt that 250 yards was the maximum safety limit they began to look thoroughly

The 'Rubber Empire' sector

jittery. It was the first time that they had been stuck so far away on their own and they had very little confidence in their military ability. They were right, too. Within ten days they had to be twice disengaged from besieging Viets—the second time it was our Company that was sent along and we were thoroughly surprised to see to what point the post, which we had left in first-class condition, had deteriorated.

The 'Rubber Empire' was only a twenty-mile flight for a crow from Suo Hiep, but it was a good forty-five miles by third-class dust tracks, and it was not till late in the afternoon that the last truck was unloaded and we had time to take in our new quarters. The 'Empire' had really done us proud. Right in the heart of the plantation there was a vast clearing, and in the clearing had been built a hospital for the coolies and other native workers. There were a dozen enormous bungalow dormitories, all with showers and lavatories, and several other smaller buildings for the staff. Five of the bungalows had been evacuated to make room for the men and three of the smaller buildings for the use of the Captain and the NCOs. There was also a huge T-shaped kitchen and refectory combined which had been divided in two so that the Company could have one half. Lawns and flower-beds abounded, and at first sight the whole set-up looked like a pleasantly run-down summer vacation resort for children. Next to the hospital was a small hamlet where lived the plantation workers for that particular section, as well as a few of the lower-grade hospital staff. They lived in revolting little two-room hovels, at least two families per hovel, and as soon as they heard we were arriving the majority had stocked up on beer and stuff to eat. A sure way to augment their incomes—the Legion was always thirsty and paid well. Our men had just been paid and for the first few days it was impossible to find one of them in the quarters—they were all guzzling beer in the village.

The 'Empire' itself was an extraordinary set-up. The head-quarters were in a small town on the Saigon River, about five miles from the hospital. To get into the 'Empire' it was necessary to cross a bridge which was controlled by a private police force who levied a tax on all incoming goods. The factories and warehouses were all there, as well as the two-storey brick houses for the European personnel. They were very large houses and were placed in enormous well-kept gardens.

The plantation workers were registered and lodged in the section where they worked, each section having its hovel hamlet. For food the coolies were supplied with rice, fish, nuoc mam, etc., by the 'Empire' at a fixed price. They were allowed a ration a head a month for their families and it was docked off their wages. Apart from food, the 'Empire' ran an enormous general store where the natives could buy on credit everything they needed, from the black cotton material for their clothes to fishhooks, native tobacco and hairpins. As their pay was slightly less than half that of a French private in Indochina, it was a fairly safe bet that they would stay sufficiently in debt to the 'Empire' to be unable to quit, and the latter always advanced them enough for feasts, funerals and marriages to keep them reasonably happy.

From a mechanical point of view the 'Empire' was the best organised affair I had seen in years. Their roads were all mac-adamised, their transport was all mechanised, their general equipment included bulldozers, scrapers, graders, earth removers, steam-rollers, mobile cranes and all the odds and ends that went with them. There were huge maintenance garages, pumping and electric generating plants powered by the latest diesels, and, as a touch of refinement, a first-class macadamised airfield with hangars and three planes, for the use of the European personnel when they wanted to drop down to Saigon or to go down to the sea for the weekend, when the 'Empire' swimming pool began to pall.

The surrounding countryside being openly hostile the 'Empire', naturally enough, needed quite a bit of protection to keep running and we weren't the only company installed on their territory. In all there must have been at least a battalion and a half of European troops, mostly Legion, and two battalions of native regulars with European officers and NCOs. The troops were scattered about at strategic spots in and around the 'Empire' and their main job was to prevent the Viet from infiltrating and ringing the trees or smashing the porcelain sap-collecting bowls.

Where things got complicated was when the Viet got into the plantation. Once they got in we had our hands tied; it was forbidden to open fire in the plantation for fear we might hurt the trees. The Viet, quite naturally, couldn't have cared less about the trees, with the result that we did our best to avoid such mani-festly one-sided actions. In general the Viet were gentlemanly about the matter and we did our best to avoid each other. From what we could gather the 'Empire' had done much the same. It was a state within a state and, on that basis, came to an unwritten agreement with the Viet who, in return for certain rights of way and revictualling facilities, agreed not to overstep the limit by fighting inside the plantation. A few bursts of tommy-gun fire could do as much damage to the trees as ten men with bleeding knives working all night.

The first few days we spent at the hospital post were slightly tense as we hadn't got into the swing of plantation morals. We posted sentinels all the way round the grounds and, still under the influence of Suo Hiep, waited for the worst to happen between sundown and sun-up. Once we had realised the difference, however, we relaxed and adopted the live-and-let-live policy which was in general favour. The results were mildly catastrophic. We had been so used to the strain of Suo Hiep that the sudden change went to our heads and the general discipline, which had never been the Company's strong point, went to the dogs.

The house put at the Captain's disposal was a three-room bungalow, with a kitchen and bathroom, set well apart from the others. Shortly after our arrival, about the 10th of January, he disappeared down to Saigon for a couple of days and came back during the siesta, while everybody was asleep. It wasn't till fairly late in the evening that we were aware that he had brought Mlle Yvette back with him. He came strolling into the mess with her, introduced her all round, ordered drinks, and announced that we would be delighted to know that she had come to stay a week. His private life was none of our business, but we didn't like having it quite so close.

The immediate result of her arrival was the sudden appearance of most of the congaies who had been left behind in Cau Chi. But there was no room for them in the hovel hamlet, so they installed themselves in odd corners of the hospital buildings. A situation so obviously untenable that it soon blew up and the Captain had them all thrown out with a formal interdiction to return. As Yvette was still staying in his bungalow, feelings ran high and discontent was general. However, since the Captain rarely appeared—the little official business he attended to Hartz or I took along to his bungalow—quite a few of the men took to leaving on the quiet for a day or two. We had nothing to do, so their absence never was noticed officially. Hartz, once he had seen the set-up at the hospital, had even decided to stay on another three months with his congaie who had come up from Cau Chi. He was in no real hurry to get back to Africa. When the Captain had the congaies thrown out, Hartz quite coolly took an unofficial week's leave and the Captain never noticed that he had been away till he came back. By then it was too late to do anything, so the matter was dropped. The slackness reached such a point that one day in mid-January we were nearly sunk by a visit from the Colonel of the Regiment, who had dropped in to see how we were getting on. The Captain ordered the Company to reassemble for inspection by the Colonel. By a superhuman effort we managed to get about half the Company together and the Captain had to do some fast talking to explain where the rest had got to.

That visit decided him to tighten up on the discipline and to get the men back on to the job, so for the next few days there were innumerable patrols in the plantation. They were soon called off once we shot up a group of auxiliaries, whom we had taken for Viets, and life went drifting on downhill. Hartz and I began to get worried, however. The Company's finances were getting into the devil of a mess and it was impossible to make the Captain do anything about it. He just didn't have the time, we had neither the cash box nor the cash register, and it took a lot of juggling to keep the creditors quiet and the Company fed.

Apart from the one day operation we made to drive the Viet away from the post at Suo Hiep (where we never actually saw the Viet, who had been warned of our approach and the siege was lifted just before we arrived) and a few plantation patrols, we had had no operation activity for nearly a month.

Quite apart from the congaie question, the Company was getting bored. We were totally unaccustomed to inactivity.

It was with relief, therefore, that we welcomed the news that the Company was needed for a three-day operation. We were to take part in a large-scale sweep down one bank of the Saigon River. The object was to stop the Viet from attacking a convoy of the 'Empire's' barges, loaded with rubber, which were Saigon-bound. At least it meant a change of surroundings, if nothing else. Living in the middle of a plantation became a stifling and hypnotic affair. The endless rows of geometrically aligned trees had a very definite effect; it made me feel as though I was in prison with a mesmerist.

At the last moment the Captain decided that I had to stay behind and look after the post and generally take over in his absence. I was furious, but there was nothing to be done but obey. The Company was due to leave at six in the morning and I went round to see the Captain at half-past five to find out if he had any further orders. He had. I was to take the jeep and driver and escort Yvette back to Saigon. He hadn't wanted to ask any-one else and felt sure that I understood. To soothe me down he said that Hartz could take over the post and that I could take a couple of days off once I had delivered her to Saigon as long as I sent the jeep straight back. I got the Captain to sign a blank leave pass before he left; forty-eight hours were worth taking, even if it did mean taking Yvette as far as Saigon.

We were in Saigon by midday and, as soon as I had dumped Yvette and sent the jeep back to the Company, I set about hunting up one or two cronies I though might be in town. I headed straight for the market place, which was about the best spot in Saigon to find people at that time of day. Most of the company trucks were usually there completing their stores before getting back. Sure enough I ran into the one man I least expected to see. Hans Schmeider and I had been in North Africa together and we had been through the same corporals' training. He had come over to Indochina shortly after I did and had been assigned to the Battalion's D Company but we had rarely been able to see each other. He had just been promoted to Sergeant and was in

Saigon on a pass to celebrate..I gave up the idea of looking for anyone else and we went off together to have a drink. Neither of us knew Saigon well and we had no fixed plans, so we decided to spend our leave together. The first thing we did was to hunt up one of the 'Bath and "Complete" Massage' establishments we had both heard about. They were apparently a thing not to be missed. Since the easiest way to find anything in Saigon was to get into a *pousse*, we hailed one and told the man to take us to the best massage place in town. After a nerve-wracking ride through the crowded streets he drew up alongside a scruffy-looking building and told us that we had arrived.

Inside it was slightly cleaner and a reasonable-looking woman took some money off us and showed us into our cubicles. Once we were undressed she led us along to a steam chamber, where we stayed for a while, then took a shower and went back to our cubicles to recover from the heat. Each cubicle had a rest couch. I was half asleep when suddenly I felt a pair of butterfly wings fluttering over my body—it was a delicious sensation and I just didn't want to stop the dream. In the end I opened my eyes and found that I was being stroked to death by an Annamite girl with a poker face. It was so damned impersonal that I told her to stop, paid what I owed, and dressed. Schmeider had had the same treatment and about the same reaction.

Vaguely disappointed, we wandered off to find a native place to eat. We felt an urge for local specialities and finally found an Annamite restaurant that looked good. We sat down and ordered prawns stewed in coconut milk with garlic, and lacquered duck with rice; for drink we picked a Chinese wine without knowing what it would be. When the food arrived we realised that we hadn't known what that would be, either. The prawns were fine but they had chopped up an entire duck, a big one, and put it in the middle of an enormous bowl of rice. It was a dish for at least six persons. To give ourselves the courage to tackle the food we decided to try the wine. Heaven alone knows what it was made of, but by the time we wiped away our tears and got our

The client had no choice

breaths back after the first glass, we felt capable of taking on anything. The prawns, the duck and the wine disposed of, we felt a lot better and badly in need of cool beer, which we found not far from the restaurant. It was then getting on for five o'clock, so we began to discuss what we would do with the rest of the evening. A hotel was easy enough to find, but it was too hot for the movies and we didn't want to get plastered. Schmeider finally suggested that we should go and see the 'Buffalo Park'. Neither of us had ever been there, but we had heard a lot about it. The Buffalo Park was *the* Forces brothel. There were hundreds of girls in there and even if we didn't want one the set-up was worth having a look at.

We stopped a *pousse* and as soon as we told the man where we wanted to go he gave a grin and suggested that he knew several better places, or could even find us high-class girls with their own apartments. Much to his disappointment, we were adamant and to the Buffalo Park we went.

Before going in we buttoned up our pockets and made sure that our wallets were secure. We also agreed to find each other at a bar just opposite, if either of us felt the urge and we had to separate. With that we went in. We hadn't even got through the double doors when we were set on by about two hundred women of every shape, size, age, colour and race imaginable. They clutched and dragged us into the middle of a vast courtyard, which was surrounded by cubicles, and set to to see which of them would get us. In the process our képis and stripe badges had been snatched off and were being used by the four women who had seized them as priority claims on our persons. Schmeider and I stood by while the four of them battled it out.

The client didn't seem to have any choice in the matter at all and we were beginning to get a bit panicky at the idea of having to taste the delights of any one of the four, or, for that matter, of the couple of hundred of others who had welcomed us. Luckily two or three innocents came in to the slaughter just then and, while the main horde swept down on the newcomers, we were left to cope with the two who had won our képis and stripe badges. It was really quite pleasant watching somebody else go through the mill. The three who had followed us must have been real men, however, because we saw them disappear into the cubicles without a murmur. We managed to get back our belongings after a little bickering and bartering and the girls finally agreed to let us alone in return for a drink. We took them into the bar, about as big as a city hall, stood them a beer and won our independence.

We had had enough of it by then, and sneaked out before we got set upon again; neither of us felt terribly rapeable now we had seen what the Buffalo Park had to offer. Once outside, we felt that we had done enough sight-seeing for the day, so we went off to a hotel, booked a couple of rooms, and turned in.

Chapter

20

SCHMEIDER AND I woke up late and, by the time we had dressed, shaved and breakfasted, Saigon was already steaming with heat like a Turkish bath. Neither of us felt very enthusiastic about spending another day and night there, so I suggested that we should get a lift as far as Loc Ninh, drop in to see my friend Thieu, have lunch with him and then go our respective ways. Schmeider was certain to get a lift back to his company from Loc Ninh and there was always a lot of traffic, both civilian and military, for the 'Empire' which passed through Loc Ninh. We soon found a truck going our way and by eleven-thirty we were in Loc Ninh.

Thieu was delighted to see me again and before we had crossed the threshold of his house we were invited to lunch. He had already eaten—like most Annamites, he had lunch around ten-thirty—but he soon had a table set for us with a mass of different dishes. He sat down with us and kept up a running stream of gossip about what had been happening in the village and in the neighbourhood. After we had eaten, Schmeider decided to get on back to his Company, so we wandered over to the Battalion HQ post and found a truck which was just ready to leave. We said goodbye and I left the post in a hurry. I was still on leave for another twenty-four hours and I had no desire to get collared by Lieutenant Dindon, or anybody else, to discuss official business. I went back to Thieu's for a drink and asked him if he could put me up for the night; he could, so I put off getting back to the 'Empire' till the next day. I spent the rest of the afternoon and evening drinking and talking with old friends from the HQ and Thyme's platoon and, once Thieu had shut up shop, turned in with pleasure.

I got up early and went across to the HQ post to see if there was any mail or official papers to take back and the first thing I was asked was if Schmeider and I had been together the day before. I said 'Yes' in a puzzled way. The man who asked me was Goellec, who had taken over the job of Battalion Sergeant-Major from me in September. We knew each other fairly well and I was sure he had something unpleasant to say. It was. Schmeider had been killed in the night along with a couple of other men in his platoon. The building in which he slept, a munition dump and a 120 mm mortar—the only one in the sector—had been blown up by plastic charges. He and two others had been killed in their sleep. The charges had been placed by someone from inside the post and fired from outside by remote control. The news had just come in with the first batch of radio messages from the Companies. Goellec gave me the Company's official mail and suggested that I come back in an hour to see if he knew anything more. I left the office feeling thoroughly sick and went back to Thieu's to have a drink. At ten o'clock I got back to the HQ office and Goellec told me what he knew. A couple of the Légionnaires in D Company had been working for the Viet for months past and it was they who had planted the charges the night before. As soon as the D Company post had opened its gates in the morning the two of them had gone into the village and tried to get away across country. A patrol had spotted them dodging through the brush, had stopped them, questioned them as to why they were alone and, getting suspicious, had been none too gentle in their questioning. The two had broken down and admitted to placing the charges, and throwing the contact wires over the defences to the Viet who were outside. The whole business stank and there was bound to be the hell of a row when GHQ got hold of the story.

With that I left Goellec and went across to Lieutenant Dindon's office to see if he wanted anything from the Company. He did; he wanted to find out what the devil was going on; we were hopelessly in the red, he never saw the Captain, neither Hartz nor I ever came down to HQ, it was already February and he hadn't yet seen the colour of our January accounts as yet, etc., etc.

I pointed out that the Captain kept everything concerning the finances in his own hands and that it was impossible for us to go anywhere as he wouldn't loan his jeep and the truck was always in use. Dindon, however, knew more than I thought. He made a couple of cracks about the Company being run by a woman and the Company's jeep being used to escort her wherever she went, which meant that official business came second. Then he got up, drew me out of the office and asked me quietly if the barmaid had become a permanent institution. C Company was becoming the laughing-stock of the sector and everybody knew that we were balancing on a financial tight rope. Primary loyalty still came first, so I tried to sidetrack the question. Dindon understood and let the matter drop. But before he went back into his office he told me to be very careful about what I signed when I took over from Hartz. I told him that I had no intention of signing anything. Hartz had never taken over officially. Since I had been in the Company I had seen far too much to want to stick my neck out. I liked Hartz personally, but he was no angel and a good deal of the mess could inevitably be traced back to him. He had been in the Company for three years, he had been there when Captain Blanche took over and he must have had a very good reason for not signing an official receipt for the Company's statements of account.

Come what may, I had no intention of doing so either, until I had been able to verify the books for myself. Lieutenant Dindon agreed and advised me to hang on as long as I could without making any definite move; he said that he would advise me when the moment was ripe and when it could be done with the least possible disturbance.

There was little enough good feeling between Captain Blanche and Lieutenant Dindon owing to the former's incorrigible arrogance and his conviction that he was the darling of the Saigon GHQ ever since he had thrown his party at Suo Hiep. He had been so caught up with the idea of the bigger men that he had never asked either the Battalion Commander or any of the other officers in the Battalion; they were small fry and of minor importance. Nevertheless, the Company was still under the administrative control of the Battalion, and Lieutenant Dindon, who controlled the finances of the Battalion, could if he liked make life very unpleasant.

Schmeider's death and Lieutenant Dindon's fireside chat had the most depressing effect on me and it was with relief that I found a truck for the 'Empire'. I hoped that the jolting of the road would help to change my ideas a bit. The truck was loaded with stores, and there were a couple of men aboard as escort as well as the NCO who was in charge. I climbed aboard and settled down on some sacks of potatoes and we started off. I was smoking and thinking of Schmeider. We must have been on the road for about half an hour, when there was a familiar roar of a mine going off and the truck jerked to a stop—still on the road and still upright. As I was digging myself out of the potatoes I heard a couple of smaller explosions and bits of metal screeching over my head. I decided to stay put in my potatoes for a while. I was unarmed and could be of no use.

After a few seconds, I realised that nothing more was happening and finally got out of the potatoes and off the truck. The driver had managed to stop as the mine went off and had a front wheel blown off; from the look of things the mine had been a small and primitive affair. The other explosions had been caused by the two men who were escort jumping off the truck into the ditch on the side of the road. They had wanted to get under cover, to fire in case there was an ambush, and had landed on top of a couple of hand grenades, unpinned and hidden in the mud by the Viet. The damage could have been worse, however; the two men escaped with multiple minor wounds from splinters; the driver, the NCO and myself with a few bruises. The truck was in a bit of a mess but repairable. Fortunately there was plenty of traffic on the road and before long a truck came along bound for Loc Ninh. We put the wounded men aboard and the driver went along with them to fetch the breakdown truck. The NCO and I stayed with the wreck till he got back and whiled away the time by drinking a bottle of beer or two from the stock he was transporting. As soon as the breakdown gang arrived I stopped another truck going towards the 'Empire' and went on my way.

By the time I got back to the hospital post it was late in the afternoon and Hartz had news that the Company would be back some time during the night. We finished off the most important part of the work in hand and got it ready for the Captain to sign before he disappeared or became inaccessible. A precautionary measure, as in the message Hartz had received the Captain had asked for the jeep to be ready to leave for Saigon early in the morning—which could only mean Yvette.

When the Company got back at ten o'clock we saw that something had gone badly wrong. The men were not only dog-tired but also in a state of barely repressed, sullen rage. As soon as the men had got off the lorries lined up and dismissed, the Captain, instead of making his usual speech, shot off into his bungalow followed by a hostile murmuring from the men. It wasn't the moment to go and see the Captain, so I went over to Schiller's room to find out what it was all about. Schiller, dead beat, was lying on his bed still fully clothed and filthy, with tears streaming down his face. I was about to leave when he asked me to stay—he said that if he didn't talk to somebody he was in such a state that he'd murder the Captain. While he pulled himself together I went round to the mess, got a bottle and went back. He had a stiff drink and, feeling better, he apologised for having let himself go and started to talk.

The operation had gone perfectly normally the first day. The Company had been allocated a section of country to sweep and had run into absolutely nothing. They had camped near the river for the night, the platoons placed at strategic points along the bank to make sure that the Viet didn't try to cross over from the other side. After a calm night they had advanced a few miles downstream and, once the convoy had passed, started back. For the return trip they were to make a semi-circular sweep away from the river bank to see if they could find any sign of the Viet.

Schiller had been sent on ahead of the Company with his platoon, the other platoons fanning out behind. The Captain had stayed with his command platoon, which was following about five hundred yards behind Schiller. For the first couple of hours all had gone well and the Viet were nowhere to be seen. Then Schiller began to smell trouble. Ahead of him he heard a tom-tom beat, then stop, three times.

Up till then they had been going through virtually dead country, there had been no sign of human life or domestic livestock, but they had just reached the limit of the brush and directly ahead of them lay cultivated paddy-fields. He sized up the situation rapidly, signalled to the men behind to halt and cover and went back to the Captain to report. He suggested to the Captain that he should keep to the brush and sweep round the cultivated U-shaped basin instead of going straight through across the dikes. The Captain agreed, but told him to stick to the edge of the brush and to use the dike that skirted the basin. Schiller didn't like the idea of having to keep his men in the open and said so. The Captain, however, maintained that there was nothing to worry about.

Schiller went back to his platoon and got them on the move again. The men liked it as little as he did and automatically closed up on each other—a normal reaction when there was trouble in the air, however inadvisable it may have been. He had advanced about halfway round, five hundred yards, when there came a series of almighty explosions from just behind him, and at the same time the dike was swept by a hail of bullets coming from the far end of the U. He had his men leap off the dike into the brush and get into firing positions. Schiller passed word on down the line to find out how many had been caught by the mines which had gone up. The answer came back— four killed and six badly wounded still on the dike. Several times volunteers tried to get back on to the dike to drag in the wounded, but each time they were driven back by the heavy and accurate Viet fire. They answered back as best they could, but they were badly placed.

Meanwhile Schiller waited for the other platoons to come up to the rescue. They should have been just about to follow him on to the dike. He was left with seven valid men including himself, two of the wounded had already been hit for a second time and killed and he and his men were pinned down. He waited for an hour before the other platoons came up through the brush and opened a concentrated fire on the Viet positions, heavy enough to make them keep their heads down and permit him to collect his dead and wounded, of whom a third had been killed. It brought his score to seven dead and three wounded, all of them badly hit. Finally, the Captain had come along and said that the Viet might have tried to spring a double trap; he hadn't wanted to risk any lives unnecessarily. He may have been right, but the effect on all hands was just the opposite; the other platoon commanders had had all their time cut out to stop the men from going off to the rescue. What really burned Schiller up was the Captain's insistence that he should take the dike instead of cutting through the brush. He had been nearly five years in Indochina. He had commanded a platoon for two years and up till then he had never had a man killed in an ambush or on a mine. His only dead had been in open combat. He knew the country, knew the

Viet and had always been able to smell out trouble before it broke.

They had picked up the dead and wounded and, with the Captain in the lead, had made a long detour round the danger zone and after several hours' march had arrived at the rendezvous fixed for the trucks. It was from there that the Captain had sent a message back to the post for his jeep, and another message to Battalion HQ to announce the losses.

I left Schiller, who felt a little better having said what he wanted to say, and dropped over to the Captain's bungalow to see if he had any orders for me. He wanted nothing, however, except to sign the papers he had to straight away, so that he could get away first thing in the morning. He told me to get the necessary papers established for the dead, gave me their names and added that he wouldn't be back the next night as he would be staying in Saigon in order to arrange for the funeral. He would send a message through as to how many men could come down for the ceremony and that was all.

Forty of us went down for the burial. We met the Captain at the cemetery and spotted Yvette hovering in the background, suitably dressed in black and dabbing her eyes. The last note of the Last Post over, we went to the trucks and started back for the 'Empire'. On the way the Captain's jeep raced by in a swirl of dust; we couldn't see who was with him. When we got back we found that it was Yvette, who had gone along to console him. The Company was stupefied. Basically we didn't give a damn what he did, but somehow that eternal woman around even when we were burying our dead, angered us. We were never very sentimental about those who had been killed; we were there for that, it was part of the Legion's job to get killed, but we preferred not to have outsiders present during our last rites.

Chapter

21

FORTUNATELY, THE CAPTAIN realised the way things were going and reacted rapidly before trouble broke out. Early in February he called a meeting of the platoon commanders, which Hartz and I attended as well, and asked us to talk freely about the rot that had set in. The meeting got off to a very slow start, nobody wanting to say what he thought. Finally it all came out and the Captain took it very well. He understood our feelings about Yvette being more or less permanently installed in his bungalow and that inactivity was ruining the men, and even understood that none of us liked the Company being the object of ridicule for the rest of the Battalion, which openly mocked us for being run and ruined by a woman. Once we had all said what we had to say, he told us that he would take the necessary steps to pull the Company together again, and added that, in return, he expected us to back him up to the hilt. He had called us together with the express purpose of hearing our views and respected us for having been honest with him. From then on we could count on him to support any decision we had to take, in our respective functions, for the general discipline and well-being of the Company. With that he declared the meeting over and we left for the mess, where we tried to figure out what was going to happen next. The general effect of his initiative, however, was good and we all felt better for having been able to say a little of what we thought. Personally, I hadn't tackled the money problem as it concerned only the Captain, Hartz and me, but I had decided to get on to the subject as soon as possible.

The Captain's first step was to send Yvette back to Saigon the same day. The second was to call another meeting the same evening. He had us into his bungalow, where we found him with a map of the region spread out on the table.

When we were all present he started to outline a plan he had cooked up during the afternoon. We were to leave the hospital at three in the morning. The men were not to be warned of the departure until an hour before, in order to avoid all risks of a leakage of information in the hovel hamlet where they went for beer. On leaving the post we would have an hour's march due west, along small tracks, to reach the nearest border of the 'Empire' territory. He showed us the route on the map and pointed out an area that was another half-hour's march from the border-line. There the country was mixed marshland and paddy-fields, controlled by the Viet and used as grazing for their buffaloes. We should be able to reach the spot an hour before dawn and place the platoons in position without having been spotted. Absolute silence and a strict no-smoking rule would be two vital essentials. The buffalo herds were normally put out to pasture at daybreak, under the care of a few small boys, a universal custom in those parts. Our job would be to surround as many buffaloes as we could, as fast as we could, and get away before the Viet had time to organise themselves. As far as possible we were not to use firearms, unless we were attacked, in order to avoid alerting the Viet. Once back to the 'Empire' boundary there would be trucks waiting to load the buffaloes, which a local butcher had agreed to buy. The profits of the expedition would be split between the Company's kitty and the men's canteen; for our mess there would be something as well. The order of the split would be a quarter for the canteen and the rest for the Company. The Captain would direct the proceedings on the spot, helped by his Annamite cook, who was an ace at handling buffaloes.

It was a genial plan and we were all for it. The Captain ran over the main points again, made sure that the platoon commanders knew where to place themselves once we had arrived, and sent us off to work out the definite role of each man. Speed would be of vital importance, as buffaloes were dangerous customers. For all their bulk they were fast runners and agile, and it was a tricky job to get a rope through their nose-rings without getting tossed. On top of it all the sight and the smell of white men were enough to make them charge. It usually took a minute or two for them to make up their minds, but once one started a charge the whole herd followed and it was the hell of a job to get away from them. Doubly so if it was open country without trees.

At two o'clock the hospital post came to life, discreetly and with the minimum of noise. The men were told to get dressed and to put on rubber sneakers. Equipment was cut to the minimum, and checked so that nothing rattled or squeaked, and the platoon commanders explained to their men what we were going to do. The effect on the men was electric—even the most bloody-minded became enthusiastic. Buffalo-rustling was something they all appreciated, and it brought in tangible results. By three everything was ready and the Company slipped out of the post by a side entrance, the Captain in the lead. We got clear of the hovel hamlet without even so much as dog barking to announce our departure. All told we were fifty strong; we had left twenty men behind in case anything happened—the rest were in hospital or away on instruction courses.

We went fast and noiselessly, cutting through the plantation on the tracks which the Captain had mapped out the evening before. The moon was high and bright and we were able to avoid the odd pitfalls along the way. I was up in front just behind the Captain and when, from time to time, I looked back along the line of men who were following I had the impression we were being tracked by ghosts. The silvery light of the moon and the lack of all noise heightened the effect. The plantation was eerie at any time; for some strange reason it was completely shunned by every form of wild life except mosquitoes, and it was only the slight sound of a man slapping at a particularly voracious mosquito which changed the ghosts back into flesh and blood.

The march down to the 'Empire' boundary went off like clockwork and we arrived on the grazing grounds on time. The last part of the way he had advanced with the greatest possible caution on account of the bullfrogs. Wherever there was water there were thousands of bullfrogs and the latter kept up their booming all through the night unless someone passed by, then stopped and wouldn't start off again until the vibration of footsteps had died away. For anyone setting an ambush they were ideal for giving the warning, and *vice versa*, which made them a mixed blessing. We settled down in the ditches which flanked the way in to the grazing grounds, camouflaged ourselves as best we could, and waited. After a while the bullfrogs picked up their chorus again and we felt more at ease; at least we hadn't been spotted on our way across the open ground.

The monotony of the wait for daybreak was broken only by the mosquitoes which, as time dragged on, began to assume the proportions of dive-bombers. We didn't dare slap at them for fear of scaring the bullfrogs and the brutes took full advantage of the fact. Their favourite pastime seemed to be to see how far they could get inside our ears and still keep buzzing before deciding to take a bite. From time to time we got a mild scare when a particularly heavy bullfrog splashed into the water from a dike. The stillness amplified the noise and made it sound like men walking through the paddy-fields; then we realised that the bullfrogs were still croaking and relaxed again. At long last the dawn began to break and we could hear the faint sounds of a village waking up in the distance, an odd cock's crow and the voices of the natives scolding their cattle. As the light increased we improved our positions as much as possible and tried to work the stiffness out of our arms and legs to be ready for the sudden effort of racing around after the buffaloes. Along the ditches there was a vague rustling as the men tightened their belts and adjusted their equipment.

I was in the same ditch as the Captain, his cook and Schiller's platoon, and it was the cook who was the first to give the warning. The sun had just started to pour up over the horizon when he nudged the Captain and whispered that he could hear the herd approaching. A minute or two later we all picked up the noise and the cook could even make out the herders talking. He said that from what he could gather there were seven or eight children and they were all laughing and joking.

Finally the first buffalo came lumbering along. From where I lay its slate-grey hulk of a body looked gigantic, and I had a momentary pang of anguish at the idea of being chased around by something that big. After it came a whole bunch of bulls, cows and calves—there must have been about sixty of them— followed by half a dozen small boys who were driving the buffaloes along by pelting them with bits of dried mud. The buffaloes must have smelled us; suddenly the whole herd stopped and turned towards the ditches where we, lay their heads up, swept-back horns lying along their backs and snorting hard through their flared nostrils.

The Captain anticipated the charge by shouting the order to surround the herd, and we all leapt up out of the ditches. The cook yelled at the children not to move and, before they could get over their surprise, they were seized, bound and laid along the bank of a ditch. The buffaloes had started to mill around, uncertain whether to charge, make a break for it or do nothing. The cook asked the Captain to get the men to stay still while he tried to get hold of what looked like the herd boss. He sidled up and was just about to slip a lead rope through his nose-ring when the brute's head went up and he flashed off with the herd at its heels. Those of us who were in their way scattered as fast as we could. Buffaloes or no, we had no intention of being run down.

The next five minutes were spent in a hectic free-for-all corrida in which we were the bulls and the buffaloes the matadors.

While the rest of us were being chased around, the cook had managed to get hold of the animal he was after and was driving it away; the other spotted their leader moving off and went lumbering after him. The rest of us, bruised, scratched and in some cases slightly gored, took up the rear. The Captain, who had been helping the cook, stood on a slight knoll to count the herd as it passed. We had managed to get twenty-three, including the calves, without a shot being fired. At least half of the herd had been able to get away from us, but for what we had received we were truly thankful and we kept our little herd on the run towards the 'Empire' boundary. By dint of prodding with sticks, pelting with stones and general harrying we made good time and reached the boundary in little over forty minutes from the beginning of the round-up. As far as we could make out, there had been no alert from the village and we were able to load the buffaloes on to the trucks without too much trouble. The animals were so blown that they offered little resistance, which was just as well; we were so blown ourselves that we wouldn't have been able to cope if they had started another corrida.

By eight o'clock we were back in the hospital and to all intents and purposes we looked as though we were coming in from a normal patrol, except for the general elation. The butcher had paid the Captain on the spot and, as soon as the men had taken off their equipment and cleaned their arms, he called all hands into the canteen, ordered the barman to open up as much beer as the men could drink in half an hour and announced that the rest of the day was free. With that he went off to change, ordered his jeep and left for Saigon, to pay the tradesmen who had been clamouring for weeks.

Later in the morning a phone call came through from Regimental HQ, which were installed in a section of the 'Empire's' European quarter. It was the Colonel's ADC who wanted to speak to the Captain. I told him that the Captain had gone down to Saigon on business and wouldn't be back till the evening. There was a brief silence and then he asked if by any chance we had seen a herd of buffaloes pass by the hospital accompanied by two or three platoons of a European unit. I replied, quite truthfully, that nothing like that had been seen in our area and he rang off. I dashed off down to the mess to tell the others and we decided that the platoon commanders had better warn their men to keep their mouths shut, at least until the Captain got back. Something must have gone wrong somewhere and we didn't know just what.

I spent the rest of the day catching up on the work in hand and was rung up another three times by the Colonel's ADC, who wanted to know if the Captain had come back. The Captain appeared about seven in the evening and I told him what had happened. He looked completely thunderstruck by the news; muttering a string of oaths, he got back into his jeep and dashed off to HQ to find out what was going on.

He came back with bad news. The native grapevine had worked faster than we thought. We had been spotted, by the village near the grazing grounds, as we were driving away the buffaloes we had managed to round up. The villagers had come along shortly after and had found the children we had left by the ditch. The children had described us fairly accurately and the village elder had passed the news on. The hovel hamlet next to the hospital had heard the news and had in turn passed it on to the 'Empire' HQ, adding that we had come back at eight in the morning looking happy but without any cattle. The real fly in the ointment was that the Captain had, knowingly or unknowingly, chosen the grazing ground of a village that was affiliated to the 'Empire' and not to the Viet. The buffaloes were all urgently needed for the work in the paddy-fields and the villagers were raising hell. At HQ the Captain had denied having any knowledge of the affair; he said that he had sent out half of the company on patrol before dawn and that they had come back with nothing to report and, for the moment, the matter was left there.

We had the cash, the butcher had his beef, and it was just too bad for the villagers.

Chapter
22

PERSONALLY, I HAD little time to enjoy the calm that followed. Hartz had left and I was busy trying to catch up with the inevitable tangle of loose ends. There was no one to replace him and I had to cope with all the mass of red tape alone. It would have been hard enough if it had been in my native tongue, but coupled to the fact that everything was in French was the added complication that one had to speak German to deal with the affairs which concerned the men. Though officially we were limited to fifty per cent of any given nationality, the company was effectively seventy-five per cent German or of Germanic origin and few of them ever bothered to learn any French.

For a while things ran fairly smoothly; then, towards the end of March just before the rains, the Company was used as the odd-job man for the sector. Every day we got orders to send a few men here and a few men there, to reinforce other units or to protect road and rail convoys. In a short while we had the Company scattered all over the place and the nightmare of ensuing paper activity began again. After a fortnight of that, the Company was suddenly brought together again and sent off to Suo Hiep. GHQ had decided to continue with its earlier projects after all. This time, however, we were not to reoccupy the post we had left, but were to push on to the Saigon River and start building a post there. It was with mixed feelings that the men took off for their second stay in the jungle. To complicate matters, it had been decided to leave the Company office at the hospital along with the men who weren't in fit marching condition. Another couple of sergeants, twelve men and I found ourselves stuck at the hospital, without so much as a truck and with a platoon of Cambodians to assure the necessary guard duties. It was the hell of a situation.

All the official papers for the Company had to go back and forth between Suo Hiep and the hospital and the resulting delays doubled the work involved. To help things along the Cambodians, who had been sent to the hospital, were on the point of laying down their arms and returning to Cambodia. They were dissatisfied with their pay and living and working conditions. With the Cambodians there was nothing much we could do if they decided to leave. They were recruited on the understanding that they could quit when they felt like it and the only way they could get into trouble for leaving was by forgetting to turn in their armament. Once, however, one of them laid down his rifle and equipment we could do nothing to stop him from going, except point out the joys of army life. In the end we managed to persuade half of them to stay and the defaulters were replaced by new men from a neighbouring outfit. It wasn't a pleasant sensation, however, to be guarded by men who might leave in the middle of the night.

Meanwhile I hadn't been able to broach the matter of the Company finances with the Captain, before he left for Suo Hiep, let alone the questions of stores and equipment which he had claimed as lost during the October cyclone, the list of which I had never seen. One day the answer to his claims arrived, accompanied by a memo from Lieutenant Dindon that the matter be reconsidered. At the same time he had added a list of all the stores and equipment which the Company ought to have. I made a rapid check and to my horror found that we had about double of everything, which, in the French Army, was a far more heinous

offence than having less than the official amount. I mustered the
few valid men left and set them to knocking together crates and
boxes in which to put the surplus and hide it wherever possible,
in case of a sudden inspection. After two days' hard work we got
most of the stuff camouflaged and I breathed easier for a while.

Bit by bit I was getting overwhelmed by everything. Physically
I was run down, and I began to find it very hard to concentrate on anything at all, spending far more time than was healthy
lost in a vague reminiscent vein. In particular I kept on coming
back to all the different people I had known in the Legion who
had met death and disaster in various forms. It was most depressing
to realise how many had fallen by the wayside. For some it had
been countless attacks of malaria or dysentery which had finally
led them to hospital and invaliding home. Others had gone under
from the combined effects of heat and alcohol. The majority,
however, had been the victims of the eternal guerilla mine-laying
activity which got them when least expected. As for myself, the
constant strain of battling with paper and petty corruption was
definitely beginning to tell.

I had few of my original friends left. Bodenko had been blown
up on a mine while coming back from patrol. Thyme was
under arrest and facing a court-martial charge for mishandling
the funds of the commando he had been put in charge of.
Schwartz, who had been one of my drinking companions and in
charge of the battalion transport, had been taken suddenly ill and
died of a ruptured liver before they could get him to hospital.
Innumerable others had been killed or wounded.

I felt desperately alone and at times apprehensive as to what
my own particular fate would be. I had the feeling of sinking
into a bottomless morass. I was surrounded by forms to be filled
in in endless quantities, by questions I couldn't answer, by
responsibilities which weren't mine and by an overwhelming
boredom with the whole damn thing. I hadn't joined the Legion
to spend my life behind a desk: I had fondly imagined that the
Indochinese war was an all-out effort to protect an innocent people

against the unwelcome attentions of the communists. I had even imagined that equity and justice were amongst the principal objectives. Not even in my wildest dreams had I realised that I was to become part of a mercenary army deliberately trained to devastate. The men of the Foreign Legion were first-class soldiers, but they had nothing whatsoever to do with a mission of pacification and political re-education. The Foreign Legion was brilliant at two things—killing and dying well, both of which the Légionnaires did frequently and with *éclat*. But that had little to do with protecting the quiet little yellow men who surrounded us, hated us cordially and occasionally got round to murdering us when they saw the chance. Whether it was the subtly corrosive influence of the 'Empire', the heat, the disgust, general fatigue, boredom or a mixture of the whole lot, I'll never really know, but the net result was that I went down with the classic *coup de bambou*. When a man suddenly collapsed for no specific reason it was known familiarly as the *coup de bambou*—I was sent down to a hospital in Saigon where I stayed in a state of utter exhaustion until I was sent back to North Africa on the hospital ship *Oregon*.

I was in very bad shape both physically and psychologically, and the two months I spent in hospital were a godsend. Without realising it, I had been running downhill dangerously fast. Quite apart from the climate, which I had come to accept as inevitable, I had fallen into the standard trap of Indochina. In order to boost my morale and energy when things weren't going well, my trips to the sergeants' mess for a drink had become far too numerous. In the mess there were always a few others in for the same purpose. Even so, we managed to get through our work and it was never till the cudgel-blow fell that one realised what was going to happen. I had seen others go the same way without ever imagining that I was to suffer the same fate.

The hospital interlude gave me time to get things back into some sort of reasonable perspective, and I was able to realise that I was totally unsuited to the particular kind of adventure into which I was launched when I committed myself to the Foreign

Legion. An admirable organisation for the desperate—but not at all the place for those who have a certain lust for life and liberty.

Just before we embarked on the *Oregon* the Chief Medical Officer of the hospital told me that I would undoubtedly be released as soon as I got back to Sidi Bel Abbes. I only had two more years of service, and by the time my leave was over it wouldn't be practical to send me back to Indochina—my health not being good enough to stand the climate any longer. It was with a high morale that I embarked—the end was at long last well and truly in sight.

The ship itself was one of the first diesel freighters ever built by the Germans, around 1927. Indescribably slovenly, constantly breaking down, it had been handed over to the French as war reparations. The wards for the walking sick and wounded were down in the holds, where we slept in triple-tier bunks. The bed cases were slightly better off in that their beds were individual, but they never saw the light of day and their only consolation was in the fact that the surgical block and medical attention were first-class. We were all mixed together, regardless of race, rank or creed, and separated only by the nature of our wounds or ailments. Those who were really badly off were the extreme psychiatric cases, who were stowed down the after-hold in a series of large heavily barred cages—their only means of seeing daylight was by coming up into a heavily screened cage, open only towards the sea. They suffered terribly from the heat through out the trip through the Indian Ocean, the Red Sea and the Suez Canal. There as in Djibouti, Port Said, Suez and Pondicherry, where we called, the cage on deck was closed and they had to stay below. The rest of us could at least stay on deck throughout the trip. Food and general conditions were good on the whole.

After a thirty-four day trip we arrived at Algiers and were taken off to hospital where those of us who could walk were given day passes. After three days, those of the Legion capable of travelling were shipped off to Sidi Bel Abbes—a terrible fourteen-hour trip through the hottest part of the day in a slow train.

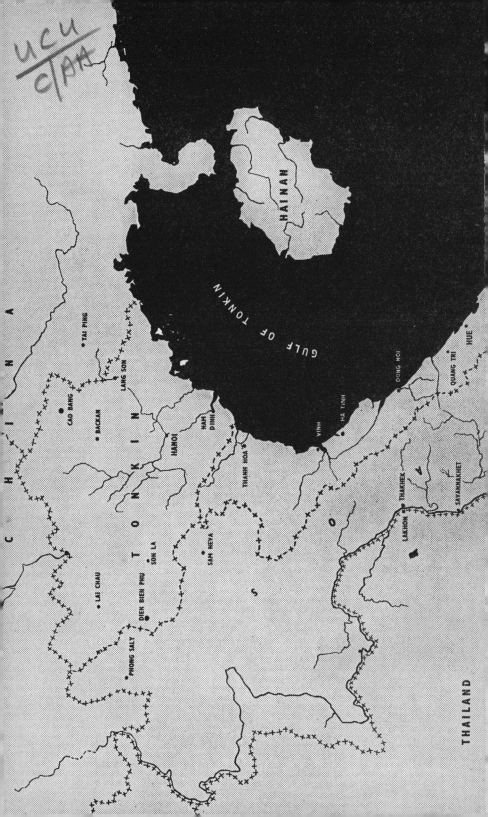

UCU
C/BA

HAINAN

GULF OF TONKIN

CHINA

TAI PING

CAO BANG

BACKAN

LANG SON

TONKIN

HANOI

NAM DINH

THANH HOA

VINH

HA TINH

DONG HOI

QUANG TRI

HUE

LAI CHAU

DIEN BIEN PHU

SON LA

PHONG SALY

SAM NEUA

LAOS

LAKHON

THAKHEK

SAVANNAKHET

THAILAND